CHESS CALCULATION TRAINING

Volume 1

Middlegames

by

Romain Edouard

Thinkers Publishing

www.thinkerspublishing.com

Managing Editor
Romain Edouard

Assistant Editor
Daniël Vanheirzeele

Software
Hub van de Laar

Proofreading
Adam Emerson, Roger Emerson

Graphic Artist
Philippe Tonnard

Cover design
Iwan Kerkhof

Back cover photo
Ana Matnadze

Typesetting
i-Press <www.i-press.pl>

First edition 2017 by Thinkers Publishing

Chess calculation training. Volume 1: Middlegames
Copyright © 2017 Romain Edouard

ISBN 978-94-9251-003-7
WD/2016/13730/8

All sales or enquiries should be directed to Thinkers Publishers, 9000 Gent, Belgium.

e-mail: info@thinkerspublishing.com
website: www.thinkerspublishing.com

TABLE OF CONTENTS

KEY TO SYMBOLS

!	a good move
?	a weak move
!!	an excellent move
??	a blunder
!?	an interesing move
?!	a dubious move
□	only move
=	equality
∞	unclear position
⯑	with compensation for the sacrificed material
⩲	White stands slightly better
⩱	Black stands slightly better
±	White has a serious advantage
∓	Black has a serious advantage
+−	White has a decisive advantage
−+	Black has a decisive advantage
→	with an attack
↑	with initiative
⇆	with counterplay
Δ	with the idea of
⌒	better is
≤	worse is
N	novelty
+	check
#	mate

PREFACE

After writing my exercise book "The Chess Manual of Avoidable Mistakes – Volume 2", I wanted to continue in the same spirit by launching another series of books: "Chess Calculation Training". This first volume will focus on middlegames.

I have always found that existing puzzle books, however good they are, only provide a rather mechanical form of mental training. In this new collection, you will find exercises to help you improve in specific areas of thinking, such as you may encounter in your own games. To help this, all the problems are taken from real games, with most of them having taken place in the last year.

The book begins with a warm-up. After that, you will find several types of exercises. Some of these fall into the same categories as those in my previous book, as they were readers' favourites. Other categories are completely new, for instance: "Find the killer positional move!" or "Find the stunning winning move!".

The problems in the book are accessible to players with a level from modest to confident. The most difficult ones are marked with an asterisk, while the most challenging chapter comes with a help page, that you may check when necessary.

I hope you enjoy solving these 496 puzzles, and look forward to seeing you again in Volume 2: Endgames.

Romain Edouard

March 1st 2017

Chapter 1

Warm up

As the title indicates, this part of the book is a warm up. For each position given, you must find the winning move. If there seem to be more than one, you should go for the quickest and/or the clearest.

This chapter contains exercises of all types, which could have been used in several of the other chapters. They have been collected in this chapter because of their lower difficulty and will prepare you nicely for the rest of the book!

This chapter is quite long: I recommend attempting one or two pages (4 to 8 exercises) as a daily routine, or as a warm-up before looking at another chapter.

📖 1

Naiditsch, A. – Mamedyarov, S.

■ 29... ? −+

📖 2

Landa, K. – Zhu, C.

□ 15. ? +−

📖 3

Sher, M. – Kamsky, G.

■ 15... ? −+

📖 4

Aronian, L. – Grischuk, A.

□ 41. ? +−

5

Edouard, R. – Zumsande, M.

□ 33. ? +−

 6

Eljanov, P. – Mamedov, N.

■ 37... ? −+

 **7**

David, A. – Petkov, V.

□ 21. ? +−

 **8**

Mamedjarova, Z. – Daulyte, D.

□ 46. ? +−

📖 9

Mastrovasilis, A. – Marechal, A.

☐ 35. ? +−

📖 10

Negi, P. – Marin, M.

☐ 42. ? +−

📖 11

Ivekovic, Z. – Grandelius, N.

■ 26... ? −+

📖 12

Naiditsch, A. – Demuth, A.

☐ 17. ? +−

📖 13

Anand, V. – Kramnik, V.

■ 23... ? –+

📖 14

Bjerke, S. – Freitag, M.

■ 37... ? –+

📖 15

Richard, R. – Pouya, I.

□ 42. ? +–

📖 16

Rasmussen, A. – Rydstrom, T.

□ 24. ? +–

📖 17

Barrero Garcia, C. – Granda Zuniga, J.

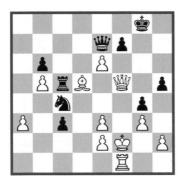

■ 35... ? −+

📖 18

Jackson, J. – Okike, D.

■ 36... ? −+

📖 19

Saric, I. – Vachier Lagrave, M.

■ 32... ? −+

📖 20

Pogonina, N. – Cramling, P.

□ 38. ? +−

📖 21

Granda Zuniga, J. – Demuth, A.

□ 22. ? +−

📖 22

Alonso, S. – Libiszewski, F.

□ 17. ? +−

📖 23

Giri, A. – Shirov, A.

□ 31. ? +−

📖 24

Ronka, E. – Edouard, R.

■ 24... ? −+

📖 25

Blomqvist, E. – Jumabayev, R.

□ 31. ? +−

📖 26

Antipov, M. – Morozevich, A.

□ 29. ? +−

📖 27

Grandelius, N. – Giri, A.

■ 40... ? −+

📖 28

Yu Yangyi – Carlsen, M.

■ 15... ? −+

Mchedlishvili, M. – Malakhatko, V.

□ 47. ? +−

Gonda, L. – Pelletier, Y.

□ 24. ? +−

📖 31

Krupenski, Y. – Gelfand, B.

□ 27. ? +−

📖 32

Abergel, T. – Vanheirzeele, D.

■ 29... ? −+

📖 33

Baskaran, A. – Abasov, N.

□ 20. ? +−

📖 34

Tomashevsky, E. – Ding, L.

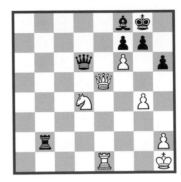

■ 53... ? −+

📖 35

Sarakauskas, G. – Howell, D.

■ 32... ? −+

📖 36

Khademalsharieh, S. – Gunina, V.

□ 62. ? +−

37

Dvirnyy, D. – Mainka, R.

□ 24. ? +−

38

Ju, W. – Zhao, X.

■ 27... ? −+

39

Cheparinov, I. – Di Berardino, D.

□ 27. ? +−

40

Kraemer, M. – Hort, V.

■ 41... ? −+

📖 41

Nisipeanu, L. – Cornette, M.

□ 24. ? +−

📖 42

Shabalov, A. – Robson, R.

■ 42... ? −+

📖 43

Degtiarev, E. – Pelletier, Y.

□ 37. ? +−

📖 44

Pantsulaia, L. – Sethuraman, S.

□ 32. ? +−

📖 45

Zatonskih, A. – Abrahamyan, T.

■ 15... ? −+

📖 46

Van Foreest, J. – Groffen, H.

□ 24. ? +−

📖 47

So, W. – Nakamura, H.

■ 27... ? −+

📖 48

Collins, S. - Short, N.

□ 16. ? +−

49

Ivanyuhin, V. – Vanheirzeele, D.

■ 16... ? −+

50

Alonso Moyano, J. – Narciso Dublan, M.

■ 34... ? −+

51

Vega Gutierrez, S. – Cramling, P.

■ 19... ? −+

52

Artemiev, V. – Inarkiev, E.

■ 37... ? −+

📖 53

Liang, A. – Landa, K.

□ 21. ? +−

📖 54

Gagunashvili, M. – Dubov, D.

■ 30... ? −+

📖 55

Riff, J. – Schlosser, P.

□ 17. ? +−

📖 56

Brunner, N. – Leroy, D.

□ 12. ? +−

57

Nisipeanu, L. – Vocaturo, D.

□ 26. ? +−

58

So, W. – Carlsen, M.

■ 28... ? −+

59

Caruana, F. – Anand, V.

□ 9. ? +−

60

Amonatov, F. – Ponomariov, R.

□ 29. ? +−

📖 61

Amonatov, F. – Artemiev, V.

□ 37. ? +−

📖 62

Kasimdzhanov, R. – Le Quang, L.

□ 19. ? +−

📖 63

Kramnik, V. – Giri, A.

□ 20. ? +−

📖 64

Aeschbach, P. – Patuzzo, F.

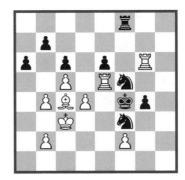

□ 45. ? +−

📖 65

Georgescu, L. – Schwander, I.

□ 25. ? +−

📖 66

Efimenko, Z. – Krasenkow, M.

□ 29. ? +−

📖 67

Bedouin, X. – Lagarde, M.

■ 28... ? −+

📖 68

Grishchenko, S. – Lagarde, M.

□ 44. ? +−

📖 69

Peralta, F. – Bachmann, A.

■ 30... ? −+

📖 70

Beukema, S. – Grandadam, P.

□ 23. ? +−

📖 71

Miralles, G. – Muheim, S.

□ 13. ? +−

📖 72

Loetscher, R. – Vernay, C.

■ 32... ? −+

📖 73

Fressinet, L. – Lorenzana, W.

□ 29. ? +−

📖 74

Giron, J. – Can, E.

■ 33... ? −+

📖 75

Congiu, M. – Berzina, I.

■ 44... ? −+

📖 76

Edouard, R. – Sosa Trani, L.

□ 30. ? +−

📖 77

Goh, W. – Duda, J.

□ 31. ? +−

📖 78

Inarkiev, E. – Yifan, H.

■ 31... ? −+

📖 79

Gelfand, B. – Giri, A.

■ 36... ? −+

📖 80

Edouard, R. – Cacho Reigadas, S.

□ 20. ? +−

📖 81

Rakhmanov, A. – Ponkratov, P.

□ 18. ? +−

📖 82

Yuffa, D. – Riazantsev, A.

□ 33. ? +−

📖 83

Karpov, A. – Timman, J.

■ 31... ? −+

📖 84

Fressinet, L. – Donchenko, A.

□ 39. ? +−

85

Socko, B. – Hoffmann, M.

□ 36. ? +−

 86

Buckels, V. – Dushyant, S.

□ 32. ? +−

 **87**

Bocharov, D. – Tomashevsky, E.

■ 38... ? −+

 **88**

Miralles, G. – Lesiege, A.

■ 30... ? −+

📖 89

Sibajeva, M. – Ambartsumova, K.

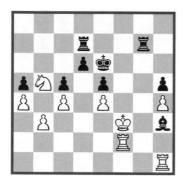

■ 68... ? −+

📖 90

Carlsen, M. – Karjakin, S.

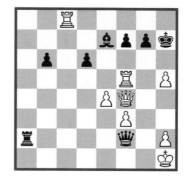

□ 50. ? +−

📖 91

Lopez Martinez, J. – Romanov, E.

■ 39... ? −+

📖 92

Ivanchuk, V. – Matlakov, M.

□ 56. ? +−

📖 93

Tregubov, P. – Moiseenko, A.

■ 22... ? –+

📖 94

Batsiashvili, N. – Kashlinskaya, A.

□ 17. ? +–

📖 95

Salomon, J. – Vachier-Lagrave, M.

■ 25... ? –+

📖 96

Stefanova, A. – Omar, N.

□ 23. ? +–

Batsiashvili N. - Kashlinskaya A.

Tregubov P. - Maisenko A.

96

95

SOLUTIONS – CHAPTER 1

📖 1

29... ♖xh2+! 0-1 Naiditsch, A [2676] – Mamedyarov, S [2728] Fuegen 2006.

White resigned in view of: 29... ♖xh2+ 30. ♔xh2 ♕h5+ 31. ♔g1 ♘e2+ 32. ♕xe2 ♕xe2 33. ♗xh7+ ♔xh7 34. ♖xf8 ♕e3+–+.

📖 2

15. c4! ♘xc4 [15... ♕f5 16. f3+–] **16. ♗xe4 ♕xe4 17. ♕xc4+–** 1-0 [19] Landa, K [2570] – Zhu, C [2501] Bad Wiessee 2006.

📖 3

15... ♘xg4! 16. hxg4 h3 17. ♗f3 ♕f6–+ 0-1 Sher, M [2420] – Kamsky, G [2705] ICC Internet 2007.

📖 4

41. ♘f6+ ♗xf6 42. ♖g7+! 1-0 Aronian,L [2750] – Grischuk,A [2726] Mexico City 2007.

Black resigned in view of: 42. ♖g7+ ♔f8 43. h8=♕#.

📖 5

33. ♖xf4! ♖xf4 34. h3 ♕g7 [34... ♕g5 35. ♕d2+–; 34... ♕f5 35. ♕g3++–] **35. ♗xf4 ♕xd4+ 36. ♔h2+–** 1-0 [39] Edouard, R [2531] – Zumsande, M [2411] Germany 2008.

📖 6

37... ♕f4+! 0-1 Eljanov, P [2720] – Mamedov, N [2594] Motril 2008.

White resigned in view of: 37... ♕f4+ 38. ♕xf4 ♘xd3+–+.

📖 7

21. ♖xc6! bxc6 22. ♘f6+ ♔g7 [22... ♔f8 23. ♕xe5+–] **23. ♘e8+ ♔f8 24. ♘xc7 ♖xe2 25. ♖xe2 ♖b8 26. ♘a6+–** 1-0 [43] David, A [2608] – Petkov, V [2490] France 2010.

📖 8

46. ♘e6+! fxe6 47. f4+ 1-0 Mamedjarova, Z [2234] – Daulyte, D [2307] Khanty-Mansiysk 2010.

Black resigned in view of: 47. f4+ ♔f5 48. ♕e5#.

📖 9

35. ♕g6+! fxg6 [35... ♖xg6 36. ♘xe7#] **36. ♘xh6#** 1-0 Mastrovasilis, A [2547] – Marechal, A [2326] France 2011.

📖 10

42. ♕xg6! 1-0 Negi, P [2661] – Marin, M [2548] Andorra 2012.

Black resigned in view of: 42. ♕xg6 fxg6 43. ♖xg7+ ♔f8 44. ♗b4++–.

📖 11

26... ♕e5! 0-1 Ivekovic, Z [2320] – Grandelius, N [2562] Athens 2012.

White resigned in view of: 26... ♕e5 27. ♖xe5 ♖d1#.

📖 12

17. ♘xc7! ♗xh2+ [17... ♔xc7 18. ♖xd6 ♖xd6 19. ♗f4+–; 17... ♗xc7 18. ♖xd8+–] **18. ♔xh2 ♖xd2 19. ♖xd2 ♔xc7 20. ♗f4+ ♔c8 21. ♘a4+–** 1-0 [25] Naiditsch, A [2724] – Demuth, A [2480] France 2013.

📖 13

23... b4! [23... ♖c2? 24. ♕xb5∓] **24. axb4 ♖c2–+** 0-1 [27] Anand, V [2773] – Kramnik, V [2793] England 2013.

📖 14

37... ♖g4! 38. ♕xg4 ♕h2# 0-1 Bjerke, S [2181] – Freitag, M [2395] Austria 2014.

📖 15

42. ♕xf6+! ♔xf6 43. ♘e8# 1-0 Rapport, R [2681] – Idani, P [2496] Reykjavik 2014.

📖 16

24. ♘f6+! gxf6 25. ♕g6+ ♔h8 [25... ♗g7 26. exf6+–] **26. ♗xf7** 1-0 Rasmussen, A [2522] – Rydstrom, T [2234] Denmark 2014.

Black resigned in view of: 26. ♗xf7 ♗g7 27. exf6+–.

📖 17

35... ♖xd5! 36. ♕xd5 ♕f6+ 37. ♔g1 ♕xf1+! 38. ♔xf1 ♘xe3+–+ 0-1 [40] Barrero Garcia, C [2358] – Granda Zuniga, J [2675] Linares 2014.

📖 18

36... ♕xd1! 37. ♖xd1 ♖xa4# 0-1 Jackson, J [2356] – Okike, D [2169] England 2014.

📖 19

32... ♕a2+! 0-1 Saric, I (2666) – Vachier Lagrave, M (2757) Wijk aan Zee 2015.

White resigned in view of: 32... ♕a2+ 33. ♔xa2 b1=♕+ 34. ♔a3 ♕b3#.

📖 20

38. ♘d7+! 1-0 Pogonina, N (2456) – Cramling, P (2495) Russia 2015.

Black resigned in view of: 38. ♘d7+ ♖xd7 (38... ♕xd7 39. ♕f6++−] 39. ♖a8++−.

📖 21

22. ♕b4! 1-0 Granda Zuniga, J (2652) – Demuth, A (2531) Andorra 2015.

Black resigned due to the double threat 23. ♕xb7 / 23. ♕f8.

📖 22

17. ♖xc6! bxc6 18. dxe5+− 1-0 (34) Alonso, S (2505) – Libiszewski, F (2543) Italy 2015.

📖 23

31. ♖d1! 1-0 Giri, A (2778) – Shirov, A (2689) Reykjavik 2015.

Black resigned in view of: 31. ♖d1 ♖xe3 (31... ♖xd1 32. ♖xc3+−] 32. ♖xd8++−.

📖 24

24... ♕xf1+! 0-1 Ronka, E (2248) – Edouard, R (2627) England 2015.

White resigned in view of: 24... ♕xf1+ 25. ♗xf1 ♖e1+−+.

📖 25

31. ♖a2! ♕xa2 (31... ♘xa2 32. ♕xa5+−] **32. ♗xa2 ♘xa2 33. ♕d2+−** 1-0 Blomqvist, E (2493) – Jumabayev, R (2599) England 2015.

📖 26

29. ♗xg7+! ♖xg7 (29... ♗xg7 30. ♕xe7+−] **30. ♖xg7+−** 1-0 (41) Antipov, M (2569) – Morozevich, A (2692) Russia 2015.

📖 27

40... ♕xe2! 0-1 Grandelius, N (2632) – Giri, A (2784) Doha 2015.

White resigned in view of: 40... ♕xe2 41. ♘xe2 ♘d2+ 42. ♔a2 ♖a8+−+.

📖 28

15... ♘xd3 16. ♕xd3 ♖e4!−+ 0-1 Yu Yangyi (2736) – Carlsen, M (2834) Doha 2015.

White resigned due to the double threat 17... ♖xa4 / 17... ♖xf4.

📖 29

47. g5! 1-0 Mchedlishvili, M (2635) – Malakhatko, V (2531) Al Ain 2015.

A simple positional kill! Black resigned in view of: 47. g5 fxe5 48. f6+–.

📖 30

24. ♘xf7! ♚xf7 25. ♘d6+ 1-0 Gonda, L (2544) – Pelletier, Y (2571) Switzerland 2015.

Black resigned in view of: 25. ♘d6+ ♚f8 26. ♗xg5 ♛xg5 27. ♗xe6+–.

📖 31

27. ♛g6+! fxg6 28. ♗g8+ ♚h8 29. ♗f7+ 1-0 Krupenski, J (2406) – Gelfand, B (2735) Tallinn 2016.

Black resigned in view of: 29. ♗f7+ ♚h7 30. hxg6#.

📖 32

29... ♖e1!

Instead, the game went: 29... f5?? 30. ♖d7⇄ ½-½ (36) Abergel, T (2475) – Vanheirzeele, D France 2016.

30. ♛xf7+ ♛xf7 31. ♖axf7 ♖xc1!–+

📖 33

20. ♖ge1! ♛h4 [20... ♖xe1 21. ♛xf2+–; 20... ♖xd2 21. ♖e8#] **21. ♛xe2+–** 1-0 (35) Adhiban, B (2653) – Abasov, N (2556) Wijk aan Zee 2016.

📖 34

53... ♖b1! 0-1 Tomashevsky, E (2728) – Ding, L (2766) Wijk aan Zee 2016.

White resigned in view of: 53... ♖b1 54. ♚g2 ♖xe1 55. ♛xe1 ♛xd4–+.

📖 35

32... ♘c3! 33. ♚f3

33. bxc3? ♗d5+ 34. ♚h2 ♖h1#

33... ♘xe2 34. ♗xe2 ♖xb2–+ 0-1 Sarakauskas, G (2415) – Howell, D (2693) England 2016.

📖 36

62. ♛xh5+! ♚e4 [62... ♗xh5 63. ♖f8++–] **63. ♛g4++–** 1-0 (67) Khademalsharieh, S (2403) – Gunina, V (2496) Tehran 2016.

📖 37

24. ♖1d3! ♛xa2 25. ♖d8 ♗d7 [25... ♗e6 26. ♖xa8 ♖xa8 27. ♛d8+ ♖xd8 28. ♖xd8#; 25... ♛b1+ 26. ♖d1 ♛b4

27. ♖xf8+ ♕xf8 28. ♖d8+−] **26. ♖xa8
♖xa8 27. ♖xd7+−** 1-0 Dvirnyy, D [2571]
– Mainka, R [2416] Gemany 2016.

📖 38

**27... ♖xb6! 28. ♖xb6 ♕a7 29. ♕c6
♖b8−+** 0-1 [32] Ju Wenjun [2558] –
Zhao, X [2506] China 2016.

📖 39

27. f6! 1-0 Cheparinov, I [2684] – Di
Berardino, D [2511] Reykjavik 2016.

Black resigned in view of: 27. f6 ♗xf6
[27... ♕d6 28. ♕d3+−; 27... ♗xg3 28.
fxe7+−] 28. ♘xf6+ ♕xf6 29. ♕xc7+−.

📖 40

41... ♖c4! 0-1 Kraemer, M [2566] –
Hort, V [2427] Switzerland 2016.

White resigned in view of: 41... ♖c4
42. ♕b3 ♖xc2+ 43. ♕xc2 ♘e3+−+.

📖 41

24. ♕h3! 1-0 Nisipeanu, L [2678] –
Cornette, M [2591] Germany 2016.

Black resigned due to the double
threat 25. ♕xh5 / 25. ♘h6+.

📖 42

42... ♘e2! 0-1 Shabalov, A [2528] –
Robson, R [2663] Saint Louis USA
2016.

White resigned in view of: 42... ♘e2
43. ♖xc7 [43. ♗xe2 ♖xc1−+] 43...
♘g1+ 44. ♔h4 ♘f3+ 45. ♔h3 ♖xh2#.

📖 43

37. ♖xf8+! 1-0 Degtiarev, E [2410] –
Pelletier, Y [2566] Switzerland 2016.

Black resigned in view of: 37. ♖xf8+
♔xf8 38. ♘c5+−.

📖 44

32. ♗xf5! gxf5 33. ♗f6+! 1-0 Pantsulaia, L [2604] – Sethuraman, S [2658]
Dubai 2016.

Black resigned in view of: 33. ♗f6+
♔xf6 34. ♕h6#.

📖 45

15... ♗c5! 16. ♕xc5 [16. ♘xc5
♕xd4+−+] **16... ♖xc5 17. ♘xc5
♕d4+−+** 0-1 [24] Zatonskih, A [2470] –
Abrahamyan, T [2342] Saint Louis USA
2016.

📖 46

24. ♘f6! 1-0 Van Foreest, J [2541] – Groffen, H [2152] Netherlands 2016.

Black resigned in view of: 24. ♘f6 ♛xd4 [24... ♛xe6 25. ♛b4++–] 25. e7#.

📖 47

27... ♘xb4! 28. ♛xb4 [28. ♘xb4 ♛d1#] **28... ♛xc2–+** 0-1 [39] So, Wesley [2773] – Nakamura, H [2787] USA 2016.

📖 48

16. ♛xh5! h6 [16... gxh5 17. ♗xh7+ ♔h8 18. ♘exf7+ ♖xf7 19. ♘xf7+ ♔xh7 20. ♘xd8+–] **17. ♘exf7 ♖xf7 18. ♘xf7+–** 1-0 Collins, S [2456] – Short, N [2686] England 2016.

📖 49

16... ♛h4! 0-1 Ivanyuhin, V [1898] – Vanheirzeele, D Hasselbacken 2016.

White resigned in view of: 16... ♛h4 17. gxh4 ♖g6+–+.

📖 50

34... ♖d2+! 35. ♔h3 [35. ♖xd2 ♛xc4 –+] **35... ♛f5+** 0-1 Alonso, J [2409] – Narciso Dublan, M [2550] Mollet del Valles 2016.

📖 51

19... ♖xc4! 20. ♘xc4 ♗d5–+ ½-½ [27] Vega, S [2375] – Cramling, P [2471] France 2016.

If White protects his Knight, Black plays 21... b5 and wins.

📖 52

37... ♘xg3! 0-1 Artemiev, V [2669] – Inarkiev, E [2686] Russia 2016.

White resigned in view of: 37... ♘xg3 38. ♛xc1 ♘e2+–+.

📖 53

21. ♘xe6! fxe6 22. ♗h5+ ♔d8 23. ♗xb6+ ♖c7 24. ♗f7 [=24. ♗g4] **24... ♔c8 25. ♗xe6 ♖d8 26. ♖xd7** 1-0 Liang, A [2410] – Landa, K [2618] Sweden 2016.

Black resigned in view of: 26. ♖xd7 ♖dxd7 27. ♖d1+–.

📖 54

30... ♘g3+! 31. ♔g1 [31. ♗xg3 ♛xh3+ 32. ♗h2 ♛g2#] **31... ♘e2+ 32. ♔f2 ♘xc1 33. ♖xe6 ♘xf1–+** 0-1 Gagunashvili, M [2569] – Dubov, D [2644] Gjakova 2016.

📖 55

17. ♗xh7+! ♚xh7

After 17... ♚f8?! the game quickly ended: 18. ♘e4 ♕e5 19. ♕g4 1-0 Riff, J [2506] – Schlosser, P [2539] Drancy 2016.

18. ♖xd8 ♗xd8 19. ♕d3++−

📖 56

12. ♗g5! ♗xf3 13. ♕d2+− 1-0 Brunner, N [2442] – Leroy, D [2289] Drancy 2016.

📖 57

26. ♖xc7+! 1-0 Nisipeanu, L [2668] – Vocaturo, D [2576] Italy 2016.

Black resigned in view of: 26. ♖xc7+ ♘xc7 27. ♘c6++−.

📖 58

28... ♕xd1+! 0-1 So, Wesley [2770] – Carlsen, M [2855] France 2016.

White resigned in view of: 28... ♕xd1+ 29. ♗xd1 ♖e1+ 30. ♚g2 ♗f1+ 31. ♚f3 ♘e5+−+.

📖 59

9. ♗xg8! ♖xg8

9... ♘d7 10. ♕b3+− ½-½ [57] Caruana, F [2804] – Anand, V [2770] Belgium 2016.

10. ♕c4+−

White is winning due to the double threat 11. ♕xc6 / 11. ♕xg8.

📖 60

29. ♘e5! ♖f6 [29... ♖xe7 30. ♘xg6++−] **30. ♘d7+− 1-0** [47] Amonatov, F [2614] – Ponomariov, R [2706] Kazakhstan 2016.

📖 61

37. ♖xd4! 1-0 Amonatov, F [2614] – Artemiev, V [2653] Kazakhstan 2016.

Black resigned in view of: 37. ♖xd4 ♕xd4 38. ♕f7+ ♚h8 39. ♘xg6#.

📖 62

19. ♕xd6! ♖xe3 [19... ♕xd6 20. ♖xe8++−] **20. ♕xd7+− 0-1** [33] Kasimdzhanov, R [2703] – Le Quang, L [2718] Kazakhstan 2016.

📖 63

20. e4! ♗xe4 [20... dxe4 21. ♗b5+ ♚f8 22. ♖xd6+−] **21. ♗xe4+− 1-0** [25] Kramnik, V [2812] - Giri, A [2782] Belgium 2016.

📖 64

45. ♖e4+! 1-0 Aeschbach, P (2249) – Patuzzo, F (2358) Flims 2016.

Black resigned in view of: 45. ♖e4+ ♔xe4 46. ♖xg4#.

📖 65

25. ♗f6+! ♘xf6 26. ♖xf8+! ♖xf8 27. ♕e7+ 1-0 Georgescu, L (2127) – Schwander, I (2182) Switzerland 2016.

Black resigned in view of: 27. ♕e7+ ♔c8 28. ♕c7#.

📖 66

29. ♖xb6! 1-0 Efimenko, Z (2655) – Krasenkow, M (2614) Warsaw 2016.

Black resigned in view of: 29. ♖xb6 ♕xb6 30. ♕xa4 ♖xa4 31. ♖c8++−.

📖 67

28... ♘xc2+! 29. ♘xc2 ♖d3+ 30. ♔e2 (30. ♔f2 ♖d2+−+) **30... ♖xg3+ 31. ♔f2 ♖d3−+** 0-1 (40) Bedouin, X (2341) – Lagarde, M (2575) France 2016.

📖 68

44. ♕e4!+− 1-0 Grishchenko, S (2441) – Lagarde, M (2575) France 2016.

📖 69

30... ♖xc5! 31. dxc5 ♕e2! 0-1 (31) Peralta, F (2588) – Bachmann, A (2649) Spain 2016.

White resigned in view of: 31... ♕e2 32. ♖f1 ♖d1−+.

📖 70

23. ♗xg7! ♗xg7 (23... ♘xg7 24. ♕xf6+−) **24. ♕xf7+ ♔h8 25. ♕f8+!** 1-0 Beukema, S (2380) – Grandadam, P (2325) Bhubaneswar 2016.

Black resigned in view of: 25. ♕f8+ ♗xf8 26. ♘f7#.

📖 71

13. ♖xd4! ♗xa4 14. ♖xd8+ ♖xd8 15. ♘xa4+− 1-0 (28) Miralles, G (2441) – Muheim, S (2153) Switzerland 2016.

📖 72

32... ♗xd4! 33. ♖xd4 ♕c1+−+ 0-1 (51) Loetscher, R (2429) – Vernay, C (2479) Switzerland 2016.

📖 73

29. ♖xg7+! ♕xg7 30. ♕xe6++− 1-0 Fressinet, L (2664) – Lorenzana, W (2239) Baku 2016.

33... ♖xd1! 34. ♖xd1 ♕xf6 0-1 Giron, J [2208] – Can, E [2565] Baku 2016.

White resigned in view of: 34... ♕xf6 35. ♕xf6 ♘g4+−+.

44... ♖d4!−+ 0-1 Congiu, M [2232] – Berzina, I [2241] Baku 2016.

30. ♖xe2! 1-0 Edouard, R [2635] – Sosa Trani, L [2051] Baku 2016.

Black resigned in view of: 30. ♖xe2 ♖xe2 31. ♕c4++−.

31. ♕xc6! ♕f8 [31... ♖xc6 32. ♖xd5+−] **32. ♖xd5** [32. ♖f1!?+−] **32... ♖xc6** [32... ♕f2+ 33. ♔h3+−] **33. ♖d8+ ♖xc4 34. ♖xf8+ ♔xf8 35. bxc4+−** 1-0 [43] Goh, W [2444] – Duda, J [2675] Baku 2016.

31... g4! 32. ♕c3 [32. ♕xg4 ♗h5−+] **32... gxh3−+** 0-1 [37] Inarkiev, E [2732] – Hou Yifan [2658] Petropavlovsk – Kamchatsky 2016.

36... ♗e5! 0-1 Gelfand, B [2743] – Giri, A [2755] Moscow 2016.

White resigned as he cannot avoid ... Qh3+ in a proper way.

20. ♘c2! ♕a5 21. ♘d5! 1-0 Edouard, R [2635] – Cacho Reigadas, S [2520] Monzon 2016.

Black resigned in view of: 21. ♘d5 ♕d8 [21... ♕xd2 22. ♘xf6++−] 22. ♗b6+−.

18. ♕h5! 1-0 Rakhmanov, A [2662] – Ponkratov, P [2589] Sochi 2016.

Black resigned in view of: 18. ♕h5 gxh5 19. ♖g3+ ♗g5 20. ♖xg5#.

33. ♕h7+! 1-0 Yuffa, D [2534] – Riazantsev, A [2651] Sochi 2016.

Black resigned in view of: 33. ♕h7+ ♘xh7 34. ♘g6+ ♔g8 35. ♗e6#.

31... ♘xb3! 32. axb3 ♖xa1 33. ♖xa1 ♖xc2 34. ♖a7 ♘f6−+ 0-1 [40] Karpov, A [2628] – Timman, J [2565] Russia 2016.

39. ♗xc6! ♗xc6 40. ♖xe6+− 1-0 [64] Fressinet, L [2676] – Donchenko, A [2581] England 2016.

36. h4! 1-0 Socko, B [2604] – Hoffmann, M [2471] Germany 2016.

Black resigned in view of: 36. h4 ♕xh4+ [36... ♕g4 37. ♕xf6+ ♕g6 38. ♕xe5++−] 37. ♖h3+−.

32. ♕xf7+! ♖xf7 33. ♖b8+ 1-0 Buckels, V [2273] – Dushyant, S [2039] Hoogeveen 2016.

Black resigned in view of: 33. ♖b8+ ♖f8 34. ♗c4++−.

38... ♖xg3! 39. hxg3 ♖f2+−+ 0-1 [42] Bocharov, D [2611] – Tomashevsky, E [2724] Novosibirsk 2016.

30... ♖xe5! 31. dxe5 ♕b6+ 32. ♔h1 ♕xc7 33. ♖xf5 ♖xe5−+ 0-1 [36] Miralles, G [2413] – Lesiege, A [2521] Menton 2016.

68... ♗g2+! 0-1 Sibajeva, M [1869] – Ambartsumova, K [2288] Novi Sad 2016.

White resigned in view of: 68... ♗g2+ 69. ♖xg2 ♖df7+−+.

50. ♕h6+! 1-0 Carlsen, M [2853] – Karjakin, S [2772] New York 2016.

This trick brought Magnus his 3rd World Championship title! Black resigned in view of: 50. ♕h6+ gxh6 [50... ♔xh6 51. ♖h8#] 51. ♖xf7#.

39... ♘e2+! 0-1 Lopez Martinez, J [2552] – Romanov, E [2622] Sitges 2016.

White resigned in view of: 39... ♘e2+ 40. ♖xe2 ♖b1+−+.

📖 92

56. ♖f8+ ♔g7 57. ♕f7+! 1-0 Ivanchuk, V (2747) – Matlakov, M (2694) Doha 2016.

Black resigned in view of: 57. ♕f7+ ♖xf7 58. R1xf7+ ♔h6 59. ♖h8#.

📖 93

22... ♕h3! 0-1 Tregubov, P (2585) – Moiseenko, A (2657) Doha 2016.

White resigned in view of: 22... ♕h3 23. gxh3 ♖g6+−+.

📖 94

17. ♘xf7! ♔xf7 18. ♕e6+ ♔f8 19. ♘g5 1-0 Batsiashvili, N (2482) – Kashlinskaya, A (2429) Doha 2016.

📖 95

25... ♗xb3! 0-1 (29) Salomon, J (2470) – Vachier Lagrave, M (2796) Gibraltar 2017.

White is lost due to the ...Qxg2+ threat.

📖 96

23. ♖xc2! 1-0 Stefanova, A (2512) – Omar, N (2369) Gibraltar 2017.

Black resigned in view of: 23. ♖xc2 ♖xc2 24. ♗e4+−.

Chapter 2

Punish bad coordination!

In this chapter, the move or idea which you must find is linked to a lack of coordination in your opponent's pieces.

Keep in mind these issues which you may be able to use to your advantage: trapped pieces, a lack of free squares, undefended or badly positioned pieces, delayed development, a fragile setup.

The difficulty of these exercises ranges from quite easy to moderately difficult, unless an asterisk indicates that the exercise is more difficult.

1

Carlsen, M. – Gudbrandsen, G.

☐ 20. ? +−

📖 **2**

Koster, R. – Landa, K.

■ 23... ? −+

📖 **3**

Topalov, V. – Gelfand, B.

☐ 27. ? +−

📖 **4**

Rozentalis, E. – Vachier Lagrave, M.

■ 26... ? −+

5

Paikidze, N. – Belenkaya, D.

□ 38. ? +−

6 [*]

Howell, D. – Feller, S.

■ 22... ? −+

7 [*]

Migot, T. – Demuth, A.

■ 15... ? −+

8 [*]

Edouard, R. – Santos Ruiz, M.

□ 29. ? +−

Savina, A. – Knott, S.

■ 27... ? ∓

Radjabov, T. – Ivanchuk, V.

□ 21. ? +−

Kramnik, V. – Radjabov, T.

□ 31. ? +−

Nakamura, H. – Caruana, F.

□ 15. ? +−

13

Rusev, K. – Negi, P.

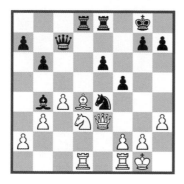

■ 24... ? –+

14

Fressinet, L. – Hammer, J.

□ 33. ? ±/+–

15

Cubas, J. – Mastrovasilis, D.

□ 45. ? +–

16

Negi, P. – Kovalyov, A.

□ 32. ? +–

📖 17

Hebden, M. – Mannion, S.

□ 20. ? +−

📖 18

Harikrishna, P. – Mamedyarov, S.

□ 27. ? +−

📖 19

Hammer, J. – Elsness, F.

□ 17. ? +−

📖 20

Jaracz, P. – Cornette, M.

■ 28... ? −+

📖 21 (*)

Mchedlishvili, M. – Parligras, M.

■ 22... ? –+

📖 22

Pelletier, Y. – Sulava, N.

□ 24. ? +–

📖 23

Ganguly, S. – Mesropov, K.

□ 23. ? +–

📖 24 (*)

Baskaran, A. – Bok, B.

□ 31. ? ±

📖 25

Van Wely, L. – Carlsen, M.

■ 37... ? −+

📖 26

Mamedyarov, S. – Hou, Y.

□ 39. ? +−

📖 27

Grandelius, N. – Sundararajan, K.

□ 38. ? +−

📖 28

Li Chao – Bachmann, A.

■ 28... ? −+

📖 29

Rathnakaran, K. – Karthik, V.

☐ 22. ? +−

📖 30

Wojtaszek, R. – Ivanchuk, V.

☐ 10. ? +−

📖 31

Mamedyarov, S. – Ding, L.

☐ 23. ? +−

📖 32

Oparin, G. – Korobov, A.

☐ 14. ? ±

📖 33

Nisipeanu, L. – Khismatullin, D.

□ 19. ? ±

📖 34

Kovalenko, I. – Fressinet, L.

□ 31. ? +−

📖 35

Sumets, A. – Naiditsch, A.

■ 45... ? −+

📖 36

Caruana, F. – Vachier-Lagrave, M.

■ 46... ? −+

37

Amonatov, F. – Potkin, V.

☐ 36. ? +−

📖 38

Wojtaszek, R. – Heberla, B.

☐ 28. ? ±/+−

📖 39

Li, D. – Libiszewski, F.

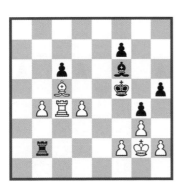

☐ 38. ? +−

📖 40

Najer, E. – Vachier-Lagrave, M.

■ 27... ? −+

📖 41 (*)

Savchenko, B. – Lomsadze, D.

☐ 43. ? +−

📖 42

Timman, J. – Kramer, J.

☐ 25. ? +−

📖 43 (*)

Jumabayev, R. – Shankland, S.

☐ 23. ? +−

📖 44

Topalov, V. – Svidler, P.

☐ 26. ? +−

📖 45

Pakleza, Z. – Sjodahl, P.

☐ 22. ? +−

📖 46

Hesham, A. – Amin, B.

☐ 26. ? +−

📖 47

Edouard, R. – Almagro Llamas, P.

☐ 12. ? +−

📖 48 [*]

Kokarev, D. – Oparin, G.

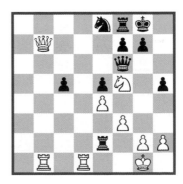

☐ 28. ? +−

📖 49

Bacrot, E. – Muzychuk, A.

□ 23. ? +−

📖 50

Frischmann, R. – Le Roux, J.

■ 25... ? −+

📖 51

Meskovs, N. – Rodshtein, M.

■ 42... ? −+

📖 52

Carlsen, M. – Karjakin, S.

■ 52... ? −+

53

Topalov, V. – Anand, V.

■ 33... ? –+

54

Zubov, A. – Gu, X.

□ 14. ? +–

55

Sheldrick, K. – Demuth, A.

■ 20... ? –+

56

Maze, S. – Lampert, J.

□ 22. ? +–

📖 57

Rapport, R. – Carlsen, M.

□ 31. ? +−

📖 58

Topalov, V. – Paehtz, T.

□ 15. ? +−

📖 59

Dek, L. – Bacrot, E.

■ 26... ? −+

📖 60

Carlstedt, J. – Oparin, G.

□ 22. ? +−

📖 61

Nakamura, H. – Iturrizaga Bonelli, E.

□ 26. ? +−

📖 62

Spraggett, K. – Milliet, S.

□ 25. ? +−

📖 63

Debashis, D. – Lagarde, M.

■ 45... ? −+

📖 64

Buhmann, R. – Vitiugov, N.

■ 29... ? −+

SOLUTIONS – CHAPTER 2

📖 1

20. ♕xa7! ♖b8 [20... ♖xa7 21. ♖xc8+ ♕d8 22. ♖xd8+ ♔xd8 23. ♘xf7++–] **21. ♕xb8! ♘xb8 22. ♖xc8+ ♔d7 23. ♖xh8 ♘c6** [23... ♕xg5 24. ♖xb8+–] **24. ♘f3+–** 1-0 [35] Carlsen, M [2072] – Gudbrandsen, G Norway 2002.

📖 2

23... ♕b7+ 24. ♖f3 ♘xc4! 25. dxc4 ♖xc3! 0-1 Koster, R [2322] – Landa, K [2597] Netherlands 2006.

White resigned in view of: 25... ♖xc3 26. ♕xc3 e4–+.

📖 3

27. ♘g4! ♕g5 [27... ♕f8 28. ♘xh6++–] **28. f4!** 1-0 Topalov, V [2780] – Gelfand, B [2737] Wijk aan Zee 2008.

Black resigned in view of: 28. f4 ♕xh5 *[28... ♕f5 29. ♘xh6++–]* 29. ♘f6++–.

📖 4

26... ♘e4! 27. ♕f3 [27. ♕xe4 ♕xf2+ 28. ♔h1 ♕xf1+ 29. ♖xf1 ♖xf1#] **27... ♕g6–+** 0-1 Rozentalis, E [2567] – Vachier Lagrave, M [2637] France 2008.

📖 5

38. ♕h2! ♕d6 [38... ♕e7 39. ♘xg6+ fxg6 40. ♕e5+ ♕g7 41. ♕b8+ ♔h7 42. ♖h1++–] **39. ♖xf7! ♖d1+ 40. ♔a2 ♕d5+ 41. c4** 1-0 Paikidze, N [2346] – Belenkaya, D [2135] St Petersburg 2010.

📖 6

22... ♘xf2! 23. ♕xc2 [23. ♖xf2 ♖xf2 24. ♔xf2 ♕b6+–+] **23... ♘h3+! 24. gxh3 ♕b6+ 25. ♔g2 ♖xc2+ 26. ♗xc2 ♖xf1 27. ♔xf1 ♕c7–+** 0-1 [48] Howell, D [2616] – Feller, S [2649] Khanty-Mansiysk 2010.

📖 7

15... g5! 16. ♖c7 ♖ac8!! 17. ♕xb7 [17. ♖xd7 ♖xc1+ 18. ♗f1 gxf4–+ Δ...♗h3] **17... gxf4–+** 0-1 [21] Migot, T [2257] – Demuth, A [2423] Belfort 2012.

📖 8

29. ♗xf6! ♘xf6 [29... gxf6? 30. ♕xh6++–] **30. ♘f5 ♕c6** [30... ♕c5? 31. ♖d8++–] **31. ♕e7+ ♔g8 32. ♘d6 ♕c5+ 33. ♔f1 ♖b8?** [33... ♗d5□ 34. ♘xc8 ♕xc8 35. ♕d6+–] **34. ♕xf7+**

♔h8 35. ♘xb7+− 1-0 Edouard, R [2641] – Santos Ruiz, M [2427] Llucmajor 2016.

📖 9

27... ♖g1! 28. ♕f4 [28. ♕xg1? ♘f3+ −+] 28... g5 29. e5 [29. ♕c1 ♕xd6−+] 29... gxf4 30. exf6+ ♔xf6∓ 0-1 [50] Savina, A [2339] – Knott, S [2322] England 2013.

📖 10

21. ♗xe5! ♗xe5 [21... ♕xe5? 22. ♖d8++−] 22. ♖d8+− 1-0 [34] Radjabov, T [2793] – Ivanchuk, V [2757] London 2013.

📖 11

31. ♗xd5 ♖xd5 32. ♖b4! ♕a2 33. ♘xe7+! ♔h8 [33... ♖xe7 34. ♕c8+ ♗f8 35. ♖b8+−] 34. ♘xd5+− 1-0 [37] Kramnik, V [2810] – Radjabov, T [2793] London 2013.

📖 12

15. ♗xd4! ♕xd4 [15... ♗xd4 16. ♕h6 ♕d6 17. ♖xd4! ♕xd4 18. ♕h7+ ♔f8 19. ♕h8+ ♕xh8 20. ♖xh8+ ♔g7 21. ♖xd8+−] 16. ♕e1+− 1-0 [34] Nakamura, H [2772] – Caruana, F [2779] Paris 2013.

📖 13

24... ♗d2! 25. ♗e5 [25. ♖xd2 ♘xd2 −+] 25... ♕d7 26. ♖xd2 ♘xd2 27. ♕xd2 ♕xd3−+ 0-1 [38] Rusev, K [2541] – Negi, P [2638] France 2014.

📖 14

33. ♘dc5! ♗xc5 34. dxc5 f5 [34... ♘d5? 35. ♘xf6++−] 35. ♕xf5 ♕d5? [35... ♖c6□ 36. ♕h5±] 36. ♕f3 [36. g4!?±/+−] 36... ♘d7 37. ♘f6+ ♘xf6 38. ♕xd5 ♘xd5 39. ♖xe6+− 1-0 [44] Fressinet, L [2709] – Hammer, J [2647] Yerevan 2014.

📖 15

45. ♗c6! [Δ♕f6] 45... ♗xc6 46. ♕f6 ♕g7 47. ♕d8+ ♕f8 48. ♖h8++− 1-0 [61] Cubas, J [2455] – Mastrovasilis, D [2608] Norway 2014.

📖 16

32. g5! ♕xg5 [32... ♕xf3 33. ♖xf3 ♗xf5 34. ♖xe8+ ♔xe8 35. gxh6+−] 33. ♗xe6 ♖f6 [33... ♖hxe6? 34. ♕xf7#] 34. ♕g4 ♕xg4 35. ♗xg4+− 1-0 [47] Negi, P [2645] – Kovalyov, A [2622] Norway 2014.

20. ♘xe5! ♛h7 [20... ♘xe5 21. ♘f4+−]
21. ♘xc6 bxc6 22. ♛xc6+− 1-0 [25]
Hebden, M [2540] – Mannion, S [2347]
England 2014.

27. ♗c7 ♖c8 28. ♗b7!+− 1-0 [35]
Harikrishna, P [2727] – Mamedyarov,
S [2765] China 2014.

Black cannot hold both Rooks on the
8th file and is inevitably losing an exchange: 28. ♗b7 ♖xc7 29. ♛xe8++−.

17. ♘g5+! ♔g8 [17... fxg5 18. ♛f3++−]
18. ♗xb7 ♛xb7 19. ♘xe6+− White is
completely winning, for example: **19...
♘f7 20. ♗xf6 gxf6 21. ♛g4+ ♘g5
22. ♘xg5 h5** [22... fxg5 23. ♛xg5+
♛g7 24. ♛d5++−] **23. ♛e6+ ♔g7 24.
♖ad1** 1-0 Hammer, J [2640] – Elsness,
F [2447] Norway 2015.

**28... ♖xh2! 29. ♔xh2 ♛h6+ 30. ♔g1
♘f3+ 31. ♔f1 ♛h1+ 32. ♔e2 ♘g1+
33. ♔d3 ♖b3+−+** 0-1 Jaracz, P [2503]
– Cornette, M [2591] Germany 2015.

22... ♖xg2+! 23. ♔xg2 ♛e8! The
Queen on a4 and the Knight on h5
are both hanging! The threat is ...c5+.
24. ♛b3 [24. ♘g3? c5+ 25. ♔g1 ♛xa4
−+] **24... ♛xh5 25. ♛xe6+ ♔f8−+** 0-1
[32] Mchedlishvili, M [2607] – Parligras, M [2584] Germany 2015.

24. ♘a4! bxa4 25. ♘c4 ♛b4 [25...
♛a6 26. ♖xa4+−; 25... ♛xb3 26.
♘xd6 ♖b6 27. ♗xc5 ♖a6 28. ♖b1+−]
**26. ♘xd6 ♖b6 27. ♘c4 ♖a6 28. bxa4
♘d7 29. a5** 1-0 Pelletier, Y [2558] –
Sulava, N [2416] Drancy 2016.

23. d5! Taking advantage of the black
Queen on b3. **23... ♘xc5** [23... cxd5
24. ♖b4+−] **24. ♖h4!+−** 1-0 Ganguly,
S [2660] – Mesropov, K [2406] Tallinn 2016. [≤ 24. ♖b4 ♘d3+ 25. ♖xd3
♗xb4 26. axb4±]

31. g4!

Instead, the game went: 31. ♗g5?
♗xg5 32. hxg5 ♗e6 33. a3↑ ½-½ [71]
Adhiban, B [2653] – Bok, B [2607] Wijk
aan Zee 2016.

31... ♗e6 32. ♗d6 ♗xh4

A) 32... ♖e8? 33. g5 ♗d8 34. ♖c2 ♕d7 *[34... ♗c4 35. b3+−]* 35. ♗c6+−

B) 32... ♖d8? 33. g5+−

33. ♗xf8 ♔xf8 34. ♖c2±

📖 25

37... ♖xf1+! 38. ♔xf1 ♖d1+ 39. ♔g2 ♗xe4−+ 0-1 Van Wely, L [2640] – Carlsen, M [2844] Wijk aan Zee 2016.

📖 26

39. ♗g4! 39... f5 [39... ♖xb8 40. ♘xc6++−; 39... ♖c7 40. ♘a6+−] **40. exf5 gxf5 41. ♖xc8 ♘xc8 42. ♘xc6+ ♔d6 43. ♗xf5+−** 1-0 [55] Mamedyarov, S [2747] – Hou Yifan [2673] Wijk aan Zee 2016.

📖 27

38. ♕e8!

Instead, the game went 38. ♗c5 ♕e6+ 39. g4± 1-0 [62] Grandelius, N [2635] – Sundararajan, K [2508] Gibraltar 2016, when in that position Black could have played 39... h5 and avoid a direct loss.

38... ♗f6 39. ♗c5

39. ♘xf6 ♕xf6 40. ♕d7 ♘e2 41. ♔g2! also wins, but is much slower and less concrete.

39... ♕e6+ 40. ♕xe6 fxe6 41. ♘xf6 ♔xf6 42. ♗d4++−

📖 28

28... ♕h2+!

The game went 28... f5? 29. ♕xc6 ♖xb6? *[29... ♕h2+ 30. ♔f1 ♖xb6 31. ♕c8+ ♔f7 32. ♕c7+ ♔g8=]* 30. ♕c8+ ♔f7 31. ♕xf5+ ♖f6 32. ♕d5+ ♖e6 33. ♕f3+ ♔g6 34. ♖d4 h5 35. c5 ♖f6 36. ♖d6± 1-0 [61] Li Chao [2751] – Bachmann, A [2610] Gibraltar 2016.

29. ♔f1 ♘f6−+ Simple chess! The white Bishop is lost.

📖 29

22. ♕c3 ♕b4 23. ♘e7+!+− 1-0 Rathnakaran, K [2463] – Karthik, V [2378] India 2016.

📖 30

10. ♗xe7+ ♘xe7 11. ♘b6! ♗e6 [11... ♕xd1+ 12. ♖xd1 axb6 13. ♖d8#] **12. ♘xa8 ♕xa8 13. c5+−** 1-0 [26] Wojtaszek, R [2727] – Ivanchuk, V [2710] China 2016.

📖 31

23. e6!

Instead, the game went: 23. axb6? axb6 24. ♕xa8 ♖xa8 25. ♖xa8+ ♘c8∞ ½-½ (39) Mamedyarov, S (2747) – Ding, L (2766) China 2016.

23... ♗xe6 (23... ♕xe6 24. ♗xe7+–)
24. ♘e5+–

📖 **32**

14. ♘c6! bxc6 (14... ♕c7? 15. ♖d8++–)
15. ♕xc6+ ♘d7 16. ♕xa8± ½-½ (37) Oparin, G (2575) – Korobov, A (2674) Gjakova 2016.

📖 **33**

19. ♗b3!

Attacking d5, and protecting b2 in case of ♘xb7 ♕xb7. Black is too badly coordinated to avoid losing one of the two pawns.

19... ♖ac8 (19... ♖ad8 20. ♘xb7 ♕xb7 21. ♕xf6±) **20. ♗xd5 ♗xd4 21. ♘xe6! ♘e5 22. ♖xe5 ♗xe5 23. ♘xf8 ♖xf8 24. ♖e1+–** 1-0 (35) Nisipeanu, L (2669) – Khismatullin, D (2609) Gjakova 2016.

📖 **34**

31. ♖1b7! ♖a1+ (31... ♕xg6 32. hxg6 ♖d1+ 33. ♔g2 ♖g4 34. ♗xc5 ♖xg6 35. ♗e7+–) **32. ♔h2 ♕xg6 33. hxg6 ♖ad1 34. ♖xd7 ♖xd7 35. ♗xc5+–** 1-0 Kovalenko, I (2644) – Fressinet, L (2692) Gjakova 2016.

Black resigned, being unable to stop 36. ♗b6.

📖 **35**

45... ♖xh2+! 46. ♔xh2 ♕h8+ 47. ♔g1 ♘e2+–+ 0-1 Sumets, A (2571) – Naiditsch, A (2663) Drancy 2016.

📖 **36**

46... ♘h3! 47. ♖xg4 (47. ♕xh3 ♘f2+ 48. ♔h2 ♕xg1#; 47. ♖g2 ♘gf2+ 48. ♖xf2 ♕g1#) **47... ♕xg4 48. ♕xg4 ♘f2+ 49. ♔g2 ♘xg4–+** 0-1 (51) Caruana, F (2804) – Vachier Lagrave, M (2789) France 2016.

📖 **37**

36. ♖f1! ♕e7 37. ♕g6++– 1-0 (39) Amonatov, F (2614) – Potkin, V (2597) Kazakhstan 2016.

📖 **38**

28. f4! ♕xf4 29. ♘e6! fxe6?! (29... ♗xe6□ 30. ♖xd8±/+–) **30. ♖xd8 ♕f2+ 31. ♔h1+–** 1-0 Wojtaszek, R (2729) – Heberla, B (2541) Poland 2016.

Black resigned in view of: 31. ♔h1 ♕xe2 32. ♕xe5+–.

📖 39

38. d5! h4 [38... cxd5 39. ♖f4+ ♔e6 40. ♖xf6++−] **39. ♖f4+ ♔g5 40. dxc6+−** 1-0 [42] Li, Di [2426] – Libiszewski, F [2542] Spain 2016.

📖 40

27... ♘c5! 28. 0-0 [28. ♕xe5? ♘xd3+−+; 28. ♖a3? ♕xd6−+] **28... ♘xd3 29. ♕xd3 ♗d7−+** 0-1 [36] Najer, E [2687] – Vachier Lagrave, M [2798] Dortmund 2016.

📖 41

43. ♘d6! ♖xd6 [43... ♖xh4 44. ♘xe8 ♖xe8 45. ♖xc7+−; 43... ♕f8 44. ♖b8+ ♕xb8 45. ♖xb8+ ♔xb8 46. ♕d8#] **44. ♕e7! ♕h8 45. ♖xa7+** 1-0 Savchenko, B [2633] – Lomsadze, D [2364] Georgia 2016.

Black resigned in view of: 45. ♖xa7+ ♔xa7 46. ♕xc7+ ♔a6 47. ♕b7+ ♔a5 48. ♕b5#.

📖 42

25. ♕d3! ♖xd3 [25... ♕xa6 26. ♕xd8#] **26. ♖a8+ ♕d8 27. ♖xd8+ ♖xd8 28. ♖xd8#** 1-0 Timman, J [2559] – Kramer, J [2341] Denmark 2016.

📖 43

23. ♕b3+!

Instead, the game went: 23. ♗h3? h5 24. ♕b3+ ♕e6 25. ♘e5+ ♔f8 26. ♕f3+ ♘ef6∞ 0-1 [63] Jumabayev, R [2613] – Shankland, S [2661] Biel 2016.

23... ♕e6 [23... ♖e6 24. ♗a1+− △♘d4; 23... ♔f8 24. ♗xg7++−] **24. ♘g5+! ♘xg5 25. ♗d5+−**

📖 44

26. ♕c3! ♘xd4□ 27. ♕xb4 ♘e2+ 28. ♔h1 1-0 Topalov, V [2761] – Svidler, P [2751] Saint Louis USA 2016.

Black resigned in view of: 28. ♔h1 ♘xc1 29. ♕b8+! ♔h7 [29... ♔f7 30. ♕xc7++−] 30. ♕b1+ ♘d3 31. ♘e1+−.

📖 45

22. ♗e4+! [22. b4? ♗xg2 23. ♔xg2 ♕b7+ 24. ♔g1 ♗e7=] **22... ♔g8 23. b4!** 1-0 Pakleza, Z [2495] – Sjodahl, P [2420] Sweden 2016.

Black resigned in view of: 23. b4 ♗xb4 [23... ♗xe4 24. ♕xe4+−] 24. ♗xb7 ♕xb7 25. ♖xb4+−.

📖 46

26. d6+ ♕f7 27. ♘f6+! 1-0 Hesham, A [2419] – Amin, B [2661] Baku 2016.

Black resigned in view of: 27. ♘f6+ gxf6 [27... ♔f8 28. ♘xh7++−] 28. ♗d5+−.

📖 47

12. ♞xf6+ ♝xf6 13. ♞g5! h6 [13…
♝xg5 14. ♝xg5 ♝xg2 15. ♝xe7+−]
**14. ♛xh6 ♝xg5 15. ♝xg5 ♝xg2 16.
cxb5!+−** 1-0 [31] Edouard, R [2635]
– Almagro Llamas, P [2436] Monzon
2016.

📖 48

28. h4! [Δ♖b6)

Instead, the game went: 28. ♛b5?
♖a2 29. ♛c4 ♖a5 30. ♛c3 ♖a2 31.
♛c4 ♖a5 32. ♛c3 ♖a2 ½-½ Kokarev,
D [2636] – Oparin, G [2617] Novosibirsk 2016.

28… ♛e6 [28… g6 29. ♖b6 ♛h8 30.
♞e7+ ♚h7 31. ♞xg6+−] **29. ♖d5! ♞f6
30. ♖b6+−**

📖 49

23. ♛xd5! ♖2xd5 24. c4 1-0 Bacrot, E
[2692] – Muzychuk, A [2561] Cap d'Ag-
de 2016.

Black resigned in view of: 24. c4 ♖c5
25. ♖xa5 ♖xa5 26. ♝c7+−.

📖 50

25… ♞xf3+!

Instead, the game went: 25… ♖fe8?
26. a3∞ 1-0 [70] Frischmann, R [2312]
– Le Roux, J [2549] Novi Sad 2016.

**26. ♛xf3 ♛h4 27. g3 ♛a4 28. ♛d3
b5−+**

📖 51

42… ♝c5! 43. ♝c3 ♖d1−+ [Δ…♚e8]
0-1 [56] Meskovs, N [2483] – Rodshtein, M [2687] Baden Baden 2016.

📖 52

52… a2! 0-1 Carlsen, M [2853] – Karjakin, S [2772] New York 2016.

White resigned in view of: 52… a2 53.
♛xa2 *[53. ♛a6 ♛d4 54. ♛xa2 ♞g4+
55. ♚h3 ♛g1 56. ♛b2+ ♚g6−+]* 53…
♞g4+ 54. ♚h3 ♛g1 55. ♛b2+ ♚g6−+.

📖 53

33… ♛b5! 34. ♛c6 ♖xf3+! 0-1 Topalov, V [2760] – Anand, V [2779] London 2016.

White resigned in view of: 34… ♖xf3+
35. ♛xf3 ♛a4#.

📖 54

14. ♞db5! ♛d7 [14… cxb5 15. ♝xd6
♛c6 16. e5+−] **15. ♝xd6 ♞e6 16. ♞a3
♝d4 17. ♞c4+−** 1-0 [39] Zubov, A [2606]
– Gu Xiaobing [2324] Sitges 2016.

20... 罩xd4! 21. 含xd4 c5+ 22. 含c4 b5+! 23. 含xb5 [23. 句xb5 皀e6#] **23... 罩b8+ 24. 含c6** [24. 含c4 含e6 25. a4 皀a6+ 26. 句b5 罩d8–+ △...罩d4#] **24... 皀xc3–+** 0-1 [25] Sheldrick, K [2151] – Demuth, A [2521] Brisbane 2017.

22. 皀b4! 句xb4 [22... 罩f7 23. 句d6±] **23. 句xf6! gxf6 24. 曑xf6++–** 1-0 [55] Maze, S [2613] – Lampert, J [2510] chess.com Internet 2017.

31. 皀c6! 罩e1+ 32. 曑xe1 曑xe1+ 33. 句f1 1-0 Rapport, R [2702] – Carlsen, M [2840] Wijk aan Zee 2017.

15. 皀xd5+! cxd5 16. 罩c7 1-0 Topalov, V [2739] – Paehtz, T [2365] Gibraltar 2017.

Black resigned in view of: 16. 罩c7 罩b8 17. 罩xb7 罩xb7 18. 曑xd5++–.

26... 皀xe3 27. 句xe3 [27. 曑xe3 罩xg2! 28. 罩xg2 曑xd1+–+] **27... 曑xh2+! 28. 含xh2 罩h6+ 29. 曑h4 罩xh4#** 0-1 Dek, L [2288] – Bacrot, E [2695] chess.com Internet 2017.

22. 句f3! 罩f6 [22... gxf3 23. 曑xh6+ 含f7 24. 曑g6+ 含e7 25. 罩h7+ 含d8 26. 曑g5++–] **23. 句fxd4+–** 1-0 [28] Carlstedt, J [2413] – Oparin, G [2625] Gibraltar 2017.

26. dxc6 罩xf1+ 27. 罩xf1 皀xc6 28. 曑f3! 1-0 Nakamura, H [2785] – Iturrizaga, E [2652] Gibraltar 2017.

Black resigned in view of: 28. 曑f3 皀xe4 29. 曑f8+ 罩xf8 30. 罩xf8#.

25. e4! 句xd4 [25... dxe4? 26. 句xe6+ fxe6 27. 曑xg5++–] **26. 曑e3! 曑f6 27. e5+–** 1-0 [37] Spraggett, K [2542] – Milliet, S [2387] Gibraltar 2017.

45... 曑b7!–+ 0-1 [48] Debashis, D [2472] – Lagarde, M [2594] Gibraltar 2017.

Black's next to move is 46... 含d7, winning an exchange.

29... 罩e1+! 30. 含xe1 [30. 句xe1 曑xf2#] **30... 皀xf2+** 0-1 Buhmann, R [2625] – Vitiugov, N [2724] Moscow 2017.

Chapter 3

Find the unexpected blow!

In this chapter, you must find unexpected incisive moves! Sacrifices, intermediate moves, surprising and hidden moves will be on the menu.

The aim of this chapter is to help you to understand how rich chess is in ideas, so that you can overcome your bad automatic reflexes. Everyone is able to spot basic things. You have to force yourself to see the rest!

The difficulty of the exercises in this chapter ranges from medium to difficult.

1

Ivanchuk, V. – Karjakin, S.

■ 16... ? ∓

2

Rozentalis, E. – Socko, B.

■ 17... ? −+

3

Guerrero, R. – Raimbault, P.

□ 18. ? +−

4

Aronian, L. – Mamedyarov, S.

■ 22... ? −+

5

Negi, P. – Idani, P.

□ 33. ? +−

6

Van Kampen, R. – Hambleton, A.

□ 22. ? +−

7

So, W. – Holt, C.

□ 24. ? +−

8

Tomashevsky, E. – Mchedlishvili, M.

□ 32. ? +−

📖 9

Korobov, A. – Swiercz, D.

■ 19... ? ∓/−+

📖 10

Hammer, J. – Schekachikhin, M.

□ 33. ? +−

📖 11

Admiraal, M. – Bok, B.

■ 30... ? −+

📖 12

Van Foreest, J. – Bok, B.

□ 29. ? +−

📖 13

Sethuraman, S. – Bai, J.

□ 40. ? +−

📖 14

Anand, V. - Aronian, L.

□ 15. ? +−

📖 15

Raykhman, A. - Heinemann, T.

■ 12... ? −+

📖 16

Harikrishna, P. - Kramnik, V.

□ 21. ? ±

📖 17

Piorun, K. – Boensch, U.

□ 27. ? +−

📖 18

Najer, E. – Timofeev, A.

□ 20. ? +−

📖 19

Watzlawek, M. – Bauer, C.

■ 8... ? −+

📖 20

Vallejo Pons, F. – Palac, M.

□ 23. ? +−

21

Moroni, L. – Parligras, M.

■ 29... ? −+

 22

Dubov, D. – Brkic, A.

□ 19. ? +−

 **23**

Fressinet, L. – Kramnik, V.

■ 22... ? −+

24

Topalov, V. – So, W.

■ 20... ? −+

📖 25

Prie, E. – Sokolov, I.

■ 25... ? −+

📖 26

Skoberne, J. – Sebenik, M.

□ 9. ? +−

📖 27

Pelletier, Y. – Studer, N.

□ 38. ? ∓

📖 28

Rozentalis, E. – Jones, G.

□ 32. ? +−

📖 29

Amin, B. – Zude, E.

□ 22. ? +−

📖 30

Carlsson, P. – Smid, M.

□ 19. ? +−

📖 31

Allen, K. – Donchenko, A.

■ 29... ? −+

📖 32

Salem, A. – Svane, R.

□ 18. ? +−

📖 33

Granda Zuniga, J. – Dominguez P., L.

□ 27. ? +−

📖 34

Kenneskog, T. – Dezelin, M.

□ 26. ? +−

📖 35

Topalov, V. – Caruana, F.

■ 36... ? −+

📖 36

Papin, V. – Ikeda, J.

□ 31. ? +−

📖 37

Lauber, A. – Zubov, A.

□ 18. ? ±

📖 38

Edouard, R. – Maiorov, N.

□ 27. ? +−

📖 39

Lu, S. – Van Foreest, J.

□ 18. ? +−

📖 40

Carneiro, V. – Fier, A.

□ 12. ? +−

SOLUTIONS – CHAPTER 3

📖 1

16... ♗xh3! 17. c4 [17. gxh3 ♕f6! 18. ♔g2 ♘h4+ 19. ♘xh4 ♕xf2+ 20. ♔h1 ♕xg3–+] **17... ♘df4 18. c5?!** [18. ♗xf4☐ exf4!?∓; 18. gxh3 ♕d7!? 19. ♗xf4 ♘xf4–+] **18... ♘xg2 19. cxb6 ♕f6 20. ♘h2 ♘xe1 21. ♖xe1 axb6–+** 0-1 [37] Ivanchuk, V [2776] – Karjakin, S [2776] Romania 2011.

📖 2

17... ♘d2! 18. ♘xc6 ♘f3+ 19. ♔h1 ♗g2+! 20. ♔xg2 ♘xe1+ 21. ♔h3 ♘xc2 22. ♘xe7+ ♔f8 23. ♗xc5 ♘xa1 24. ♘c6+ ♔e8 25. ♘xd8 ♔xd8–+ ½-½ [55] Rozentalis, E [2592] – Socko, B [2636] Austria 2012.

📖 3

18. ♕xf8+! ♔xf8 19. ♘g6+! fxg6 [19... ♔g8 20. ♖e8+ ♔h7 21. ♘f8+ ♔g8 22. ♘e6++–] **20. ♗a3+ ♘e7 21. ♖xe7 axb3** [21... ♕xe7 22. ♖d8#] **22. ♖xc7+ ♔g8** [22... ♖xa3 23. ♖d8#] **23. ♖d8+ ♔h7 24. ♗b2!** 1-0 Guerrero, R [2258] – Raimbault, P [1931] Barcelona 2012.

Black resigned in view of: 24. ♗b2 h5 25. ♖xg7+ ♔h6 26. ♖d6+–.

📖 4

22... ♖xd6! 23. ♕xd6

The game continued 23. ♕b3 ♗d5–+ 0-1 [26] Aronian, L [2803] – Mamedyarov, S [2757] Beijing 2013.

23... ♕e4!–+

📖 5

33. ♖e8! 1-0 Negi, P [2640] – Idani, P [2502] Sharjah 2014.

Black resigned in view of: 33. ♖e8 ♖xe8 34. ♕d7++–.

📖 6

22. ♖xg6! fxg6 23. ♖xe6! ♕c4 24. ♘xg6 ♔c8 [24... ♖e8 would not help: 25. ♖xe8+ ♔xe8 26. f7++–]. **25. ♘xf8 ♘xf8 26. ♖e8+ ♔b7 27. f7+–** 1-0 [30] Van Kampen, R [2631] – Hambleton, A [2468] Netherlands 2014.

Also winning would be, for example: 27. ♖xa8 ♔xa8 28. ♕xh5+–.

📖 7

24. Rxf6! gxf6 [24... Rxe2 25. Rxf8++−] **25. Bxf6+ Rxf6** [25... Kg8 26. Bc4++−] **26. Qxe8+ Kg7 27. Qe4+−** 1-0 (41) So, Wesley (2762) – Holt, C (2559) ICC Internet 2014.

📖 8

32. Nxf7! Rf8 [32... Qxf7 33. dxe6+−] **33. dxe6+−** 1-0 (34) Tomashevsky, E (2743) – Mchedlishvili, M (2618) Reykjavik 2015.

📖 9

19... Nb3+!

The only important move to see.

20. Kb1□

A) 20. Nxb3? Qxa2−+

B) 20. axb3? Qa1+ 21. Kc2 Qxb2+ 22. Kd3 Bf5+ 23. Ne4 Qxb3#

20... Nxc5 21. dxc5 Rad8!

In the game, Black went for the less precise: 21... f6∓ 0-1 (35) Korobov, A (2713) – Swiercz, D (2646) Doha 2015.

22. Bg2 Qa4 [Δ...Bf5+, ...Na5] **23. Ka1 Na5 24. Rd3 Qxf4−+**

📖 10

33. Qd7! Rxc2 [33... dxe5? 34. Rc7+−] **34. Rxc2 Qd8** [34... dxe5? 35. Rc7+−] **35. Qf7+!**

In the game White played the less precise: 35. Qxb7?! dxe5 36. Rc7 Nd6±/+− 1-0 (52) Hammer, J – Schekachikhin, M Sweden 2015.

35... Kh8 36. Rc7 Rg8 37. Ng6+! hxg6 38. Qxg6 Qe8 39. Rf7 Ng5 40. Qh5+ Nh7 41. Bd3+−

📖 11

30... Nxf2! 31. Rxf2 Re1+ 32. Nf1 Rxf1+! 33. Kxf1 Qd1# 0-1 Admiraal, M (2441) – Bok, B (2607) Wijk aan Zee 2016.

📖 12

29. Rxg7! Kxg7 30. Rg1+ Kf6 [30... Kh8 31. Rg5 Qh6 32. Rg8++−] **31. Rg5 Qh6 32. e5+! dxe5** [32... Ke7 33. exd6++−] **33. Qxe5+ Ke7 34. Qc7+ Kf6 35. Qd4!+−** [Δ Qe5+, Nf5+] 1-0 (39) Van Foreest, J (2541) – Bok, B (2607) Netherlands 2016.

35. Nh2 would also win: 35... Qxh4 36. Qe5+ Ke7 37. Rh5 Qf2 38. Qc7+ Kf6 39. Ng4++−.

📖 13

40. ♕e7+! ♖xe7 [40... ♕xe7 41. dxe7+ ♔g8 42. ♖d8+−] **41. dxe7+ ♕xe7 42. ♖xe7+−** 1-0 (69) Sethuraman, S [2639] − Bai, J [2507] Gibraltar 2016.

📖 14

15. ♘xh6! ♔xh6 [15... gxh6 16. ♕xf6+−] **16. ♕h3+ ♔g6** [16... ♘h5 17. g4+−] **17. ♖f3 ♘h5 18. ♖f5! ♘f6** [18... ♖h8 19. ♕g4++−] **19. ♕h4** 1-0 Anand, V [2784] − Aronian, L [2792] Zurich 2016.

📖 15

12... ♖xe2+! 13. ♔f1 [13. ♔xe2 ♕e8+ 14. ♔d1 ♗xb5−+] **13... ♕e8−+** 0-1 [20] Raykhman, A [2414] − Heinemann, T [2459] Germany 2016.

📖 16

21. ♘xb6!

Instead, the game went: 21. ♗xf6 ♘xf6= 0-1 [39] Harikrishna, P [2763] − Kramnik, V [2801] Norway 2016.

21... exf3

A) 21... ♗xb2 22. ♕xb2 ♘xb6 23. ♕xb6±

B) 21... exd3 22. ♗xf6 ♘xf6 23. ♘xc8 ♗xf3 24. gxf3 ♕xc8 25. ♕e5±

C) 21... ♕xb6 22. ♗xf6 ♕xf6 23. ♖xb7+−

22. ♘xc8 fxg2 23. ♖fd1 ♗xc8 24. ♗e4! By far the strongest. **24... ♘e5 25. f4 ♘g4 26. ♗xf6 ♘xf6 27. ♗xg2±**

📖 17

27. ♗xb6! ♖xb6 [27... ♕xb6 28. ♗d5+ ♗e6 29. ♗xe6+ ♖xe6 30. ♕f7+ ♔h7 31. ♖d3+−] **28. ♗d5+ ♗e6** [28... ♔h7 29. ♕h4#] **29. ♗xe6+ ♖xe6 30. ♕xf8+ ♔h7 31. ♖f7+−** 1-0 Piorun, K [2591] − Boensch, U [2552] Germany 2016.

For example White could also win playing 31. ♖d3!?+−.

📖 18

20. ♘xf5! exf5 21. ♖xh7+! ♔xh7 22. ♕h5+ ♔g7 23. ♕xf7+ ♔h6 [23... ♔h8 24. ♖xd7+−] **24. ♕xf6+ ♖g6 25. ♕h4+ ♔g7 26. ♕e7+ ♔h6 27. ♖xd7 ♕xc4** White has many wins here, for example: **28. ♕h7+ ♔g5 29. ♖d4+−** 1-0 Najer, E [2681] − Timofeev, A [2598] Russia 2016.

📖 19

8... ♘xe4!! 9. ♘xe4 d5 10. cxd5 [10. ♘c3 d4−+] **10... ♗b4 11. ♘c3 ♗xd5 12. f3 ♕f6 13. ♗b2 0-0-0−+** 0-1 [18] Watzlawek, M [2106] − Bauer, C [2634] Netherlands 2016.

📖 20

23. ♘xc5 dxc5 [23... ♖xh6 24. ♘xa6+−] **24. d6! ♗xd6** [24... ♕xd6 25. ♖xh8 ♖xh8 26. ♗xb5+−] **25. ♖xf6+−** 1-0 [28] Vallejo Pons, F [2700] – Palac, M [2577] Gjakova 2016.

📖 21

29... ♖f2! 30. ♖xf2 [30. ♔xf2 ♕xh2+ 31. ♔f3 ♖f7+ 32. ♔g4 ♕h5#] **30... ♖xe1+ 31. ♖f1 ♘e3!** 0-1 Moroni, L [2443] – Parligras, M [2599] Gjakova 2016.

White resigned in view of: 31... ♘e3 32. ♖xe1 ♕g2#.

📖 22

19. ♗a6! gxf3 [19... bxa6 20. ♘xc6+−] **20. ♗xb7+ ♔b8 21. ♗xc6+ ♔c8 22. ♗b7+ ♔b8 23. ♗xf3+ ♔c8 24. ♗b7+ ♔b8 25. ♗c6+** [25. ♗d5+!? ♔c8 26. ♗c4+−] **25... ♔c8 26. ♖b2!?** [Δ♖hb1] 1-0 Dubov, D [2644] – Brkic, A [2584] Gjakova 2016.

📖 23

22... ♘xh3! 23. gxh3 ♖xf3 24. ♖e2 [24. ♕xf3? e4+−+] **24... ♖af8−+** 0-1 [34] Fressinet, L [2687] – Kramnik, V [2812] France 2016.

📖 24

20... ♘xe4! 21. ♘xg4 [21. ♗xd8 ♘xf2+−+] **21... ♘xc3!**

Instead, the game went: 21... ♘xf2+? 22. ♗xf2 ♗xf2 23. ♘xf2 ♖xf2∓ 0-1 [42] Topalov, V [2761] – So, Wesley [2770] Belgium 2016.

22. ♗xd8 ♘xd1 23. ♗xc7 ♘b2−+

📖 25

25... ♖xb3! 26. axb3 ♘xb3+ 27. ♔d1 ♘xd2 28. ♔xd2 ♖b2+ 29. ♔d3 [29. ♗c2 ♗a4 30. ♖c1 a2−+] **29... e4+−+** 0-1 [31] Prie, E [2481] – Sokolov, I [2635] Saint-Quentin 2016.

📖 26

9. ♗a6! bxa6 [9... ♕b6 10. ♗xb7 ♕xb7 11. ♗xd6+−] **10. ♕xc6++−** 1-0 Skoberne, J [2572] – Sebenik, M [2530] Bled 2016.

📖 27

38. ♕xg6 fxg6 39. ♖f5! ♘b8 [39... gxf5? 40. f7±] **40. f7 ♘d7 41. f8=♕ ♘xf8 42. ♖xf8∓** and White is worse but definitely able to fight for a draw: ½-½ [68] Pelletier, Y [2557] – Studer, N [2462] Flims 2016.

32. ♖xd5! cxd5 33. ♕d7 d4 [33... ♗h6 34. ♕xd5+ ♔h8 35. ♘e5+−] **34. ♗xd4 ♗h6 35. ♕d5+ ♔h8 36. ♘e5 ♖xe5 37. ♗xe5+−** 1-0 [58] Rozentalis, E [2552] – Jones, G [2650] Warsaw 2016.

22. ♗xd5! ♕xd5+ [22... ♘xd5 23. ♖fg4+−] **23. ♘e4 23... ♔h8** [23... ♘xe4 24. dxe4+−; 23... ♖xe4 24. dxe4 ♕e5 25. ♕g5! ♘e8 26. f6+−] **24. ♖xg7 ♖g8 25. ♖xg8+ ♘xg8 26. f6+−** 1-0 [74] Amin, B [2654] – Zude, E [2403] Denmark 2016.

19. ♖g4! ♕xe2 20. ♖xg7+ ♔h8 21. ♖g8+! 1-0 Carlsson, P [2436] – Smid, M [2214] Prague 2016.

Black resigned in view of: 21. ♖g8+ ♔xg8 22. ♖g1+ ♗g3 23. ♖xg3#.

29... ♕xf3+! 30. ♔xf3 ♘xd5 31. ♕xd6?! [31. ♖xd5 ♗xd5+ 32. ♔f4 h6 33. g5 ♖e4+ 34. ♔f3 ♖d4+ 35. ♔e2 c3 36. ♕xc3 ♖e4+−+] **31... ♘c3+!? 32. ♔f4 ♖xd6 33. ♖xd6 ♗e5+ 34. ♔g5 ♘e4+−+** 0-1 [37] Allen, K [2236] – Donchenko, A [2581] England 2016.

18. ♘f6+! 18... ♘xf6 [18... gxf6 19. ♕g3+ ♔h8 20. ♗xa5+−; 18... ♔h8 19. ♕h4+−] **19. ♕xc5+−** 1-0 [30] Salem, A [2650] – Svane, R [2552] England 2016.

27. ♕xf6+! ♔xf6 28. h7 ♖xc1+ [28... ♖c8 29. ♖g8+−] **29. ♔xc1+−** 1-0 [56] Granda Zuniga, J [2648] – Dominguez Perez, L [2736] Mexico City 2016.

26. ♗xg6! ♕xd4 27. ♗xh7+! ♔xh7 28. ♖xd4+− [△♖h4#] 1-0 Kenneskog, T [2332] – Dezelin, M [2220] Novi Sad 2016.

36... ♖e8!! 37. ♖xb7+

A) 37. ♕xe8 ♕c1+ 38. ♕e1 d2−+

B) 37. ♘xb2 ♖xe1+ 38. ♔xe1 cxb2 39. g8=♕ b1=♕+ 40. ♔d2 ♕c2+ 41. ♔e3 ♕e2+ 42. ♔f4 d2−+

37... ♕xb7 38. ♕xe8 ♕b1+ 0-1 Topalov, V [2760] – Caruana, F [2823] London 2016.

White resigned in view of: 38... ♕b1+ 39. ♕e1 c2 40. g8=♕ ♕xe1+ 41. ♔xe1 c1=♕#.

31. ♕xh6+!! 1-0 Papin, V (2466) – Ikeda, J (2375) Melbourne 2016.

Black resigned in view of: 31. ♕xh6+ ♚xh6 32. ♖h1+ ♚g7 33. ♖h7+ ♚f8 34. ♖xd8++−.

18. ♗xe6!!

Instead, the game went: 18. ♗xe5? ♕xe5 19. ♖d4 ♗c6 20. ♖cd1 ♖ac8 ½-½ Lauber, A (2421) – Zubov, A (2606) Sitges 2016.

18... fxe6

18... ♗xf4 19. exf4 ♗c6 20. ♖e7±

19. ♕g4 ♗f5

19... ♖ae8 20. ♕h4 h5 21. ♕g5+−

20. ♕h4 (△♕e7) **20... ♖f7**

21. ♖xf7 g5!?

21... ♚xf7 22. ♗xe5 ♕xe5 23. ♖c7+!+−

22. ♕xg5+ ♚xf7 23. ♗xe5 ♕xe5 24. e4+−

27. ♖xd7! ♖xd7 28. ♖xd7 ♚xd7 (28... ♕xd7 29. exf6+−) **29. ♕d2+ ♚c8 30. exf6 e5** (30... ♖d8 31. ♗xc7 ♖xd2 32. f7+−) **31. fxg7** 1-0 Edouard, R (2613) – Maiorov, N (2500) Roquetas 2017.

Black resigned in view of: 31. fxg7 ♕xg7 32. ♕d6+−.

18. ♗xg7! ♚xg7 19. f6+! ♘xf6 (19... ♗xf6 20. ♘f5+ ♚h7 21. ♘xd5+−) **20. ♘f5+ ♚h7 21. ♘xe7 ♕xe7 22. ♕xf6+−** 1-0 (42) Lu Shanglei (2612) – Van Foreest, J (2612) Wijk aan Zee 2017.

12. ♘xh6+! gxh6 13. ♖xf6 ♗xc3

13... ♕xf6 14. ♘xd5 ♕d6 15. ♗f4+−

14. ♖xh6 ♗b4 15. ♕d3

Instead, the game went: 15. e4 dxe4 16. ♗xe4 ♖e8 17. ♖h8+ ♚g7 18. ♖h7+ ♚g8 19. ♖h8+ ½-½ Carneiro, V (2426) – Fier, A (2581) Rio de Janeiro 2017 (19. ♕f3! ♕xd4+ 20. ♗e3+−).

15... f5 16. ♕f3+− (△♕h5)

Chapter 4

Play the right move under pressure!

In each exercise in this chapter you are under pressure from your opponent. You must find the only move, or simply the best response, depend-
ing on the problems you are facing.

A short introduction to each exercise will set you on the path to the
solution. The aim of this chapter is to prepare you for difficult situations:
being under attack, needing to find resources, time pressure...

The difficulty of the exercises in this chapter ranges from medium to
very difficult, the most challenging ones being marked with an asterisk.

📖 1

Negi, P. – Zhukova, N.

■ 22... ?
Black has one move to stay fully in the game, can you spot it?

📖 2

Korobov, A. – Negi, P.

■ 23... ?
Find the drawing move!

📖 3

Mateo, R. – Demuth, A.

□ 28. ?
Black is threatening ...♛a2: but White has a way to keep the dynamic balance. Find it!

📖 4

Vega Gutierrez, S. – Videnova, I.

■ 15... ?
It looks like Black is running into big problems, but in fact he is completely fine! Can you find how?

5

Jones, G. – Melia, S.

■ 24... ?
White has a deadly threat ♘xe7+.
How can Black save the day?

6 [*]

Negi, P. – Enkhbat, T.

■ 33... ?
Black is facing a terrible attack but
he is actually winning: can you find how?

7 [*]

McDonald, N. – Hawkins, J.

■ 22... ?
White wants to play ♕h4 with the idea
♖h3: can you find the only way for
Black to defend himself?

8

Bauer, C. – Baron, T.

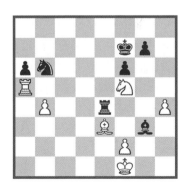

■ 55... ?
How can Black avoid losing a piece?

📖 9

Grigoryan, K. – Cuenca Jimenez, J.

■ 35... ?
Find the only move
to stay in the game!

📖 10

Fridman, D. – Kazakovskiy, V.

■ 28... ?
How can Black avoid
standing much worse?

📖 11

Fridman, D. – Gunina, V.

■ 47... ?
Can you spot what is, by far, the most
precise move in order to make a draw?

📖 12

Iturrizaga Bonelli, E. – Goryachkina, A.

■ 38... ?
Black is three pawns down but
has one move to make the
position unclear: spot it!

📖 13

Gunina, V. – Bachmann, A.

■ 37... ?
Black is a clear pawn down...
Find the best move!

📖 14 (*)

Edouard, R. – Walter, S.

■ 35... ?
Black is under a deadly ♕g6 threat.
35...♗d6?! is a draw after 36.♕d1.
Find the only way to a clear advantage!

📖 15

Wojtaszek, R. – Harikrishna, P.

■ 24... ?
Black is up a piece: but he has only one
move to be winning, can you spot it?

📖 16

Hou, Y. – Muzychuk, M.

■ 18... ?
Black is on the verge of losing:
how can he force a draw?

📖 17

Salem, A. – Sjugirov, S.

□ 40. ?
Life is no fun: Black's main threat
is 40...♖d8. Which move enables
White to stay in the game?

📖 18

Studer, N. – Demuth, A.

■ 44... ?
What move would you have
chosen as Black?

📖 19 (*)

Caruana, F. – Nakamura, H.

■ 14... ?
White sacrificed a piece, but it
didn't work. Can you spot why?

📖 20

Nepomniachtchi, I. – Aleksandrov, A.

■ 21... ?
Your clock shows 5 seconds.
Play a move!

📖 21 (*)

Vassallo Barroche, M. – Libiszewski, F.

□ Here White lost on time without being able to complete the move 57.h6. Would that move have been played, how could Black have saved the day?

📖 22 (*)

Bogdanov, E. – Bailet, P.

■ 22... ?
White has sacrificed Queen for Rook and a devastating attack. How can Black counter this attack?

📖 23

Fressinet, L. – L'Ami, A.

■ 20... ?
Your Knight on d5 is pinned on the a2-g8 diagonal and is about to be double-pinned on the d-file: how do you escape?

📖 24 (*)

Hertneck, G. – Vocaturo, D.

■ 46... ?
Find the only move to stay in the game!

📖 25 [*]

Gunina, V. – Girya, O.

■ 46... ?
White intends ♘g3-♘h5:
find the only way to defend yourself!

📖 26

Nakamura, H. – Anand, V.

■ 26... ?
The Bishop on g4 and the pawn on g5
are hanging. Your King also lacks protection. Find the – by far – best reaction!

📖 27

Postny, E. – Shyam, S.

■ 16... ?
Black is up three pawns but is losing material back... Find the best reaction!

📖 28 [*]

Nguyen, N. – Anton Guijarro, D.

■ 17... ?
Find the move granting
Black a nice advantage!

Harutjunyan, G. – Edouard, R.

■ 30... ?
Black can reach a drawish position:
find how!

Eljanov, P. – Wojtaszek, R.

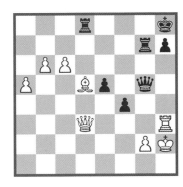

■ 40... ?
White's pawns are running fast!
How can Black save half a point?

Steinberg, N. – Svidler, P.

■ 38... ?
White plans ♗f6: it's going wrong
for Black! Save the day!

Hou, Y. – Ju, W.

□ 32. ?
Black has several devastating threats.
White to move and draw!

SOLUTIONS – CHAPTER 4

📖 1

22... ♔f8!!

Other moves are failing:

A) The game went: 22... ♘f8? 23. ♖xd8 ♖axd8 24. ♕h5+ ♔g8 25. exf6+– 1-0 (52) Negi, P (2641) – Zhukova, N (2426) Gibraltar 2012.

B) 22... ♗c8? 23. ♕xh7+ ♔f8 24. ♕h8+ ♔f7 25. ♕h5+ ♔f8 26. exf6+–

C) 22... ♖e7? 23. exf6 ♘xf6 24. ♖xd8 ♖xd8 25. ♖f1 ♖d6 26. ♕xh7+±

23. ♕xh7

A) 23. ♖xd7?? ♗c8!–+

B) 23. e6 ♖e7⇆

23... ♖e7 24. ♕h8+ ♔f7=

📖 2

23... ♕h4!

Other moves are failing:

A) The game went: 23... ♕h5? 24. ♕xe5+ ♔d7 25. ♖d2 ♖e8 26. ♕xe8+ ♔xe8 27. ♖xc2+– 1-0 (45) Korobov, A (2702) – Negi, P (2641) New Delhi 2012.

B) 23... ♔d7? 24. ♗xe5 ♕xf5 25. ♕f4! ♕xf4 26. ♗xf4 ♖e8+ 27. ♔f1 ♖ee2 28. ♗g3±

24. ♕xh4

24. ♗xe5?? ♕e4+–+

24... ♘f3+ 25. ♔f1 ♘h2+=

📖 3

28. f5!

Instead, the game went: 28. dxe7?? ♕a2 29. ♖de1 ♕xb2+ 30. ♔d1 ♕b1+ 31. ♘c1 ♘e3+ 0-1 Mateo, R (2413) – Demuth, A (2478) Rochefort 2014.

28... gxf5 29. dxe7

29. ♖xh8 ♖xh8 30. dxe7 is also OK.

29... ♕a2??

Now Black should play 29... ♘e5 with an unclear game.

30. e8=♕+! ♖axe8

30... ♔xe8 31. ♖xh8++–

31. ♕xc7++–

📖 4

15... ♗f5! 16. g4 f6!! 17. ♕d2

17. gxf5? g5−+ (△...♘f7)

17... ♗e6∞ ½-½ (63) Vega, S (2405) – Videnova, I (2379) Warsaw 2014.

📖 5

24... ♖d8!∓

Black is better since 25. ♘xe7+? is met by 25... ♕xe7 26. ♕xe7 ♖xd1+ 27. ♔h2 ♗xh6−+. That example was also seen in "The Chess Manual of Avoidable Mistakes – Volume 2".

Instead, the game went: 24... ♗xh6? 25. ♕xh6 ♖d8 26. ♘f6+ exf6 27. exf6 ♖xd1+ 28. ♔h2 ♕b8+ 29. g3 1-0 Jones, G (2671) – Melia, S (2473) Gibraltar 2015.

📖 6

33... ♗g5!!

Other moves are failing:

A) The game went: 33... ♗xg7?? 34. ♘xe6! (△♖xg7+, ♕h7#) 34... fxe6 35. ♖xd8+ ♔f7 36. ♕g6+ ♔e7 37. ♖e8+ ♔d6 38. ♕xe6+ ♔c5 39. ♖g5+ ♔d4 40. ♖d5# 1-0 Negi, P (2669) – Enkhbat, T (2417) USA 2015.

B) 33... ♖xc2? 34. ♗xf6+ ♔f8 35. ♖xc2+−

34. ♕xc4□

34. ♖xg5 ♖xc2−+

34... ♕xc4

34... ♕xd2 35. ♕xa4 ♔xg7∓

35. ♗f6 ♔h7! 36. ♖h2+ ♔g6 37. ♗xd8 f6−+

📖 7

22... ♕a7□

Instead, the game went: 22... a4 23. ♕h4 axb3 24. ♖h3 h6 25. gxh6 ♕c7 26. c3 ♖a4 27. ♖d4 ♖xd4 28. ♕xd4 f6 29. hxg7 ♔xg7 30. ♕g4++− ½-½ (51) McDonald, N (2417) – Hawkins, J (2569) England 2015.

23. ♕h4 ♕f2□∞

📖 8

55... ♘c4!

Instead, the game went: 55... ♗xf2? 56. ♔xf2 ♖xb4 57. ♖xa6+− ½-½ (78) Bauer, C (2626) – Baron, T (2544) England 2015.

56. ♘xg3 ♖g4!= (△...♘xa5 / ...♘xe3+)

📖 9

35... ♕e7□

The game went: 35... ♖d1+? 36. ♖xd1 ♕xd1+ 37. ♔h2 ♗e7 38. ♖xf6+ ♗xf6 39. ♕xf6+ ♔g8 40. ♕e6+ ♔f8 41. ♗e7+ ♔g7 42. ♕f6+ ♔h7 43. ♕f7+ ♔h6 44. ♗f8+ 1-0 Grigoryan, K (2602) – Cuenca Jimenez, J (2514) Spain 2016.

36. ♕xc5

36. ♕f5? ♖xg5 37. ♕xg5 ♕xe4∓

36... ♖d1+ 37. ♖xd1 ♕xc5 38. ♖xf6+ ♔e8 39. ♖f5 ♖xg5□ 40. ♖xc5 ♖xc5∞

📖 10

28... ♘xf3!

Other moves are failing:

A) 28... fxg3? 29. ♗xe5+− 1-0 (33) Fridman, D (2624) – Kazakovskiy, V (2387) Tallinn 2016.

B) 28... d6?! 29. ♗xe5 f5 30. ♖xf4±

29. ♖xe8 ♘h4+ 30. ♔g1 ♖xe8 31. ♕xe8 ♘f3+ 32. ♔g2

32. ♔h1 ♕h5 33. ♔g2 ♘h4+=

32... ♘h4+ 33. ♔h1 ♕d3! 34. ♔g1 ♕f3 35. gxh4 ♕g4+=

📖 11

47... ♕h2+!

A) The game went: 47... ♕f4? 48. ♕xf4 ♘xf4 49. ♖d7± 1-0 (69) Fridman, D (2624) – Gunina, V (2496) Tallinn 2016.

B) 47... ♘xe3? 48. ♖xd6++−

48. ♔xh2 ♘xe3 49. ♖d7

A) 49. ♖d6+ ♖f6=

B) 49. ♖e1 ♘xg2 50. ♔xg2 ♖f7=

49... ♖f2 50. ♔g3 ♖xg2+ 51. ♔f3 ♖xb2 52. ♔xe3 ♖b3+ 53. ♔d4 ♖xh3 54. ♖xa7 ♖h4=

📖 12

38... ♘c6!

The most important was to find this move, and to understand that the position gets terribly complicated. Other moves lead to a lost position:

A) Instead, the game continued: 38... ♖xc1? 39. ♖xc1 ♕e2 40. ♕g2+− 0-1 (61) Iturrizaga Bonelli, E (2624) – Goryachkina, A (2502) Gibraltar 2016;

B) 38... ♗e5 39. ♕g1+−.

39. ♕g5

39. ♘xc6? ♖g8∓

39... ♕f3+

39... ♕h3!? is also possible.

40. ♕g2 ♕h5

One possibility for the game to continue would be:

41. ♘xc6 ♖f2 42. ♘xd4 ♖xg2 43. ♔xg2 ♕g4+ 44. ♔f1 ♕xd4 45. ♖xc2 ♕d3+ 46. ♔e1 ♖xc2 47. ♖c1 ♕e4+ 48. ♔d1 ♔g7=

📖 13

37... ♘d4! 38. ♖xd4 ♕xf2+ 39. ♔h1

39. ♕g2? ♕xd4−+

39... ♕f1+ 40. ♔h2 ♕f2+ 41. ♔h1 ♖c1+!

Black is even better!

42. ♖d1 ♕f5! 43. ♗e1□ ♕xd5+ 44. ♖xd5 ♖xe1+ 45. ♔g2 ♖e2+∓

½-½ (67) Gunina, V (2496) – Bachmann, A (2610) Gibraltar 2016.

📖 14

35... ♗h4!!

A) The game went: 35... ♗g5?? 36. ♕g6 ♕c1+ 37. ♔g2 1-0 Edouard, R (2630) – Walter, S (2402) Germany 2016.

B) As mentioned in the instructions, 35... ♗d6?! is not convincing: 36. ♕d1 ♗c7 37. ♕d4 ♕c2 [37... ♕c1+ 38. ♔g2=] 38. ♗xg7+ ♔h7 39. ♕xg4 ♗xh2+ 40. ♔h1 ♕f5 41. ♕xf5+ exf5 42. ♗xh6=.

36. ♗g3

36. ♕g6? ♗xf2+ 37. ♔xf2 ♕f3+ 38. ♔e1 ♕xe3+−+

36... ♕d7∓

Or: 36... ♗xg3 37. hxg3 b6∓.

📖 15

24... ♖e7!

Simple but smart!

Instead, the game went: 24... ♖xe6? 25. dxe6+ ♕xe6 26. ♗b3 ♗d5 0-1 Wojtaszek, R (2727) – Harikrishna, P (2753) China 2016. White lost on time or accidentally resigned in that blitz game, but after 27. ♗xd5 ♘xd5 28. ♕h5+ the position would be close to equal.

25. ♕f3

25. ♗b3 ♔f8−+

25... ♕b4

25... ♕d8!? 26. ♗b3 ♖d7∓ (Δ...♔g8)

26. ♗b3 ♔e8!−+ White fails to prove any compensation.

📖 16

18... ♗c5!

18... ♖h1+ 19. ♔g2 ♗c5 would also do – in spite of a lack of logic!

19. ♕xc5 ♖h1+ 20. ♔g2 ♖h2+! 21. ♔g1

21. ♔xh2?? ♕h4+ 22. ♔g2 ♕h3+ 23. ♔g1 ♕h1#

21... ♖h1+= ½-½ Hou Yifan [2673] – Muzychuk, M [2554] Lviv 2016.

📖 17

40. ♖a3! [Δ♖a8].

Black is only slightly better.

Instead, the game went 40. c5? ♖d8 and White resigned as he couldn't avoid ...♕e5 next: 0-1 Salem, A [2615] – Sjugirov, S [2667] Russia 2016.

📖 18

44... ♖b2!

The rest loses! The trap was not to answer 44... ♖b1?? when White would win with 45. ♕e4!+− [Δ♖a8].

45. ♕c5 ½-½ Studer, N [2438] – Demuth, A [2550] Switzerland 2016.

White could have played on with 45. ♖a1!? ♖xf2+ 46. ♔g1 ♖f5 47. ♕e4 but he is only slightly better.

📖 19

14... ♗g4! 15. ♗xf6

15. ♕g3 ♕d7 is very likely to transpose to the game soon.

15... ♕d7! 16. ♕g3 ♔xf6

White is far from having enough compensation, for example:

17. d4 exd4 18. e5+ ♔e7 19. ♘e4 ♖ag8 20. ♘f6 ♕f5?!

20... ♘xe5!! could have been an awesome finish: 21. ♘xd7 ♗xd7 22. ♕f4 ♖g4−+.

21. ♗d3 ♕e6 22. b4 ♗a7−+ 0-1 [32] Caruana, F [2804] – Nakamura, H [2787] Paris 2016.

📖 20

21... ♔f8!=

21... ♖f8?? 22. ♕xb8 1-0 Nepomniachtchi, I [2719] – Aleksandrov, A [2577] Kazakhstan 2016. Black resigned in view of 22... ♖xb8 23. ♖e8+ ♖xe8 24. ♖xe8#.

📖 21

57. h6 ♕d3+!

57... b1=♕? fails to 58. h7+ ♕xh7 59. ♕d8+ ♔g7 60. ♕e7++−.

58. ♔h4 ♕d7!=

The position is a draw, as after 59. h7+ Black goes 59... ♕xh7+ 60. ♘xh7 b1=♕.

22... ♗h3!

In the game, Black played 22... d3+? Which is losing: 23. ♔h1 dxc2 *[23... ♗h3 no longer works: 24. ♖xg7+ ♔f8 25. gxh3 ♕e2 26. ♖f7+ ♔e8 27. ♘g7+ ♔d8 28. cxd3 ♕xd3 29. ♖e1+–]* 24. ♖af1 ♗f5 25. ♖xg7+ ♔f8 26. ♖f7+ ♔e8 27. ♗h4+– 1-0 Bogdanov, E [2269] – Bailet, P [2500] Plancoet 2016.

23. ♖xg7+

23. gxh3?? ♔h8 24. ♖xg7 ♕e3+–+

23... ♔f8 24. ♖f1+

24. gxh3 ♕e3+! The reason why ...d3+ should not be included! 25. ♗f2 *[25. ♔g2 ♕e2+–+; 25. ♔f1 ♕f3+–+]* 25... ♕g5+–+

24... ♔e8

Black is winning. For example:

25. gxh3

25. ♘f6+? ♔d8 26. ♖g8+ ♔e7 27. ♘xd5+ ♔e6 28. ♘f4+ ♔d7 29. ♖xa8 d3+ 30. ♔h1 dxc2 31. ♖d8+ ♔xd8 32. g7 ♗xg2+ 33. ♘xg2 ♕d5–+

25... d3+ 26. ♔h1 ♕e2 27. ♖gf7□ d2!? 28. ♘f6+ ♔d8 29. ♖f8+ ♔e7 30. ♘xd5+ ♔d7 31. ♖8f7+ ♔c8 32. ♘c3 ♕c4–+

20... ♖b8! [△...bxc3]

The game went: 20... ♔h8?? 21. ♖ad1+– 1-0 [32] Fressinet, L [2676] – L'Ami, A [2322] England 2016.

21. cxb4 ♖xb4 22. ♕a2 ♔h8 23. ♖fd1

23. ♗xe5 ♖e4=

23... ♕b8=

46... ♖g7□

The game went: 46... ♘fe4? 47. ♖xh4 ♖f2 48. ♖h8+ *[△ 48. ♗c2 ♖xc3 49. ♖h8+ ♔e7 50. ♖xa8 ♘xb1 51. ♔xf2+–]* 48... ♔e7 49. d6+! ♔xe6 50. ♖h6+ ♔f5 51. fxe4+ ♔g5 52. ♔xf2 ♔xh6 53. ♕d3+– 1-0 [69] Hertneck, G [2476] – Vocaturo, D [2600] Berlin 2016.

47. ♗xf6

After 47. ♖xh4? ♘ge4! 48. ♖h8+ ♔e7! it's even White who is in trouble.

47... ♕a5! 48. ♗xg7+ ♔xg7 49. ♕xb7+

49. ♔h2 ♖xg2+ 50. ♔xg2 ♕d2+ 51. ♗e2 ♕xe2+ 52. ♔g1 ♕e3+=

49... ♔f6 50. ♕f7+ ♔e5 51. ♕g7+ ♔d6 52. ♕d7+ ♔e5=

📖 25

41... ♘d2□

41...♕b6? 42. ♘g3 ♕d8 43. ♘h5 ♗xe5 44. f6 1-0 Gunina, V (2525) – Girya, O (2450) Khanty-Mansiysk 2016.

42. ♘g3 ♘c4 43. ♘h5

43. ♗xc4?? dxc4+ 44. ♔f2 g4–+

43... ♘xe5 44. dxe5 d4+ 45. e4 ♕c1=
With a perpetual check to come.

📖 26

26... ♗h5!

26... ♖xe4? doesn't do the job: 27. ♘xe4 ♕g6 *(27... ♕xd4 28. ♕xg5+ ♔f8 29. ♕h6+ ♔e7 30. ♗c2 ♗e6□ 31. ♕h4+ ♔f8 32. ♖d1 ♕g7 33. ♘g5 ♗g8 34. ♘e4 is crushing.)* 28. ♘f6! ♕xf6 29. ♖xf6 ♔xf6 30. ♕c3 ♗d7 31. d5+ ♖e5 32. ♗e4+– 1-0 (43) Nakamura, H (2779) – Anand, V (2779) London 2016.

27. ♕xg5+ ♕g6▨

📖 27

16... ♘d5! (16... ♘xa4? 17. ♘axc4 ♕b4 18. ♖cb1+–) **17. ♗xd5 exd5 18. ♖ab1 ♕b4! 19. ♖xb4 axb4 20. ♘axc4 dxc4 21. ♘xc4 ♗e6∞** 0-1 (42) Postny, E (2620) – Shyam, S (2532) Sitges 2016.

📖 28

17... ♘e7!

17... ♘g4? is not as good: 18. ♕d2! h5 19. ♗xf8 ♕d5 20. ♖g2 ♔xf8 *(20... ♕xf3! 21. ♗d6 ♔h7∞)* 21. fxg4+– 1-0 (35) Nguyen Ngoc Truong Son (2629) – Anton Guijarro, D (2650) Doha 2016.

18. ♕xd3

18. ♗xf6+ ♘g6 19. ♗xd8 dxc2∓

18... ♘g6∓

📖 29

30... ♗g5!

≤ 30... ♗d8? 31. fxe3± 1-0 (37) Harutjunyan, G (2437) – Edouard, R (2613) Roquetas de Mar 2017.

31. ♗xg5 ♗h3 32. gxh3 ♕xg5+ 33. ♔h1 ♕d5+ 34. f3!? d3 35. ♖e7 ♖a8!

35... e2 36. ♖xe2 dxe2 37. ♕xe2±

36. ♕xa8+

36. ♕c4 e2▨

36... ♕xa8 37. ♖xe3 d2 38. ♖d1 ♕xa2 39. ♖d3 ♕a5 40. R1xd2 ♕f5=

The white King's position is too weakened. The position is a draw.

📖 30

40... e4! 41. ♕xe4 f3! 42. ♕xf3 ♖xd5

42... ♕e5+ first is also fine.

43. c7 ♕e5+ 44. ♖g3 ♖xg3 45. ♕xg3

45. c8=♕+?? ♖g8+–+

45... ♕h5+ 46. ♕h3 ♕e5+= ½-½ El-janov, P (2755) – Wojtaszek, R (2750) Wijk aan Zee 2017.

📖 31

38... ♗d4+□ 39. ♔h1 ♖f3□ 40. ♖d1

40. ♖xf3?? ♕b1+–+

40... ♕f7

Now it is White who should play the only moves!

41. ♖dg1□ ♗xg1 42. ♗f6+□ ♖xf6 43. ♖xg8+ ♕xg8 44. ♕xf6+ ♕g7= ½-½ Steinberg, N (2486) – Svidler, P (2748) Gibraltar 2017.

📖 32

32. f6! (△♕f8+)

32. ♕d5?? d3! 33. ♕xd3 ♘b4! 34. ♕e4 ♕g1+ 35. ♕e1 ♕g2 36. ♕e4 *(36. ♕e2 ♕h1+ 37. ♕e1 ♕b7–+)* 36... ♕d2+ 0-1 Hou Yifan (2651) – Ju Wenjun (2583) Gibraltar 2017.

32... ♕b2+□ 33. ♔d1 ♕b1+ 34. ♔e2 ♕xc2+ 35. ♔f3 ♕d3+ 36. ♔f2=

Due to the ♖h8+ threat, Black does not have more than a perpetual check.

Chapter 5

A devastating attacking move!

In this chapter, you are on the attack. In each exercise, you must find an incisive move to destroy your opponent's defence: a sacrifice, a combination, a stunning attacking move or any other ambitious move which is devastating to the opponent's King.

One important piece of advice: do not necessarily look for artificial solutions, sometimes the move may be simple.

This chapter will help you to develop your sense of initiative and to improve your calculation skills.

The difficulty of these exercises ranges from medium to difficult. An asterisk indicates that the exercise is more difficult than average.

📖 1

Nataf, I. – Kozul, Z.

■ 36... ? −+

📖 2

Vachier Lagrave, M. – David, A.

□ 27. ? +−

📖 3

Abergel, T. – Vachier Lagrave, M.

■ 29... ? −+

📖 4

Seegert, K. – Hartl, D.

□ 14. ? +−

5

Gashimov, V. – Gelfand, B.

□ 14. ? +−

 6 [*]

Jobava, B. – Grischuk, A.

■ 50... ? −+

 7

Carlsen, M. – Radjabov, T.

■ 49... ? −+

 8 [*]

Rapport, R. – Rogic, D.

□ 26. ? +−
Hint: the mating idea must be
prepared with a clever move!

📖 9 (*)

Negi, P. – Potkin, V.

■ 18... ? −+

📖 10 (*)

Negi, P. – Adhiban, B.

□ 16. ? +−

📖 11

Kamsky, G. – Karjakin, S.

□ 69. ? +−

📖 12

Negi, P. – Portisch, L.

□ 23. ? +−

📖 13

Kramnik, V. – Fridman, D.

□ 29. ? +−

📖 14

Vishnu, P. – Negi, P.

□ 27. ? +−

📖 15

Vachier Lagrave, M. – Batchuluun, T.

□ 27. ? +−

📖 16 [*]

Grischuk, A. – Karjakin, S.

□ 32. ? +−

17

Hammer, J. – Burmakin, V.

□ 28. ? +−

18

Motylev, A. – Najer, E.

■ 27… ? −+

19

Vachier Lagrave, M. – Hammer, J.

□ 31. ? +−

20 [*]

Iturrizaga, E. – Zhang, Z.

■ 78… ? −+

📖 21

Velikic, A. – Guichard, P.

□ 19. ? +−

📖 22 [*]

Vishnu Prasanna V – Lenderman, A.

□ 15. ? +−

📖 23

Morozevich, A. – Antipov, M.

□ 32. ? +−

📖 24

Wyss, J. – Kunin, V.

□ 16. ? +−

📖 25

Adams, M. – Giri, A.

☐ 23. ? +−

📖 26

Grandelius, N. – Sundararajan, K.

☐ 43. ? +−

📖 27

Pabalan, R. – Goncalves, J.

☐ 24. ? +−

📖 28

Tissir, M. – Cornette, M.

☐ 36. ? ±

📖 29

Koneru, H. – Ju, W.

■ 10... ? ∓

📖 30

Batsiashvili, N. – Gunina, V.

■ 28... ? −+

📖 31

Movsesian, S. – Tomashevsky, E.

□ 39. ? +−

📖 32

Socko, M. – Krush, I.

□ 37. ? +−

📖 33 [*]

Ju, W. – Khotenashvili, B.

☐ 53. ? +−

📖 34 [*]

Karjakin, S. – Caruana, F.

☐ 37. ? +−

📖 35 [*]

Edouard, R. – Fridman, D.

☐ 25. ? +−

📖 36 [*]

Vallejo Pons, F. – Wynn, Z

☐ 21. ? +−

📖 37

Gagare, S. – Kuzubov, Y.

☐ 16. ? +−

📖 38

Fressinet, L. – Turner, M.

☐ 15. ? +−

📖 39

Najer, E. – Jakovenko, D.

☐ 21. ? +−

📖 40

Turov, M. – Movsesian, S.

■ 45... ? −+

📖 41

Safarli, E. – Muradli, M.

☐ 21. ? +−

📖 42

Nisipeanu, L. – Kozul, Z.

☐ 28. ? +−

📖 43

Bacrot, E. – Kogan, A.

☐ 44. ? +−

📖 44 (*)

Vachier-Lagrave, M. – Anand, V.

■ 26... ? −+

45

Karjakin, S. – Onischuk, V.

□ 43. ? +−

46

Kramnik, V. – Aronian, L.

□ 27. ? +−

47

Donchenko, A. – Hacker, J.

□ 25. ? +−

48 [*]

Bilguun, S. – Dragun, K.

□ 24. ? +−

📖 49

Fedorchuk, S. – Moussard, J.

■ 23... ? –+

📖 50 (*)

Sargissian, G. – Khademalsharieh, S.

■ 27... ? –+

📖 51 (*)

Zanan, E. – Laznicka, V.

■ 32... ? –+

📖 52

Korobov, A. – Sutovsky, E.

□ 21. ? +–

53

Kovchan, A. – Nezad, H.

□ 14. ? +−

 54

Stephan, V. – Lagarde, M.

■ 31... ? −+

 **55 (*)**

Stupak, K. – Bok, B.

■ 21... ? −+

 **56**

Wang, Y. – Mareco, S.

■ 33... ? −+

📖 57 (*)

Li, C. – Short, N.

□ 34. ? +−

📖 58

Hou, Y. – Jackson, J.

□ 31. ? +−

📖 59

Zeller, F. – Georgiadis, N.

□ 21. ? +−

📖 60

Hou, Y. – Short, N.

□ 29. ? +−

61

Caruana, F. – Nakamura, H.

□ 30. ? +−

 62

Wei, Y. – Rapport, R.

□ 26. ? +−

📖 63 [*]

Van Foreest, J. – Liang, A.

□ 18. ? +−

📖 64

Svane, R. – Mamedov, R.

□ 17. ? +−

📖 65

Radjabov, T. – Bortnyk, O.

□ 20. ? +−

📖 66

Mamedyaov, S. – Korobov, A.

□ 35. ? +−

📖 67 [*]

Jobava, B. – Atabayev, M.

□ 18. ? +−

📖 68

Salem, A. – Ivanchuk, V.

□ 22. ? +−

69

Dubov, D. – Dominguez Perez, L.

□ 19. ? +−

 70

Chu, W. – Bellahcene, B.

□ 46. ? +−

📖 71

Safarli, E. – Donchenko, A.

□ 17. ? +−

📖 72

Forcen Esteban, D. – Vazquez Igarza, R.

■ 31... ? −+

📖 73

Harikrishna, P. – Adhiban, B.

□ 40. ? +−

📖 74

Giri, A. – Andreikin, D.

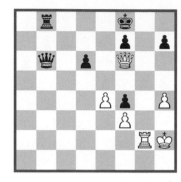

□ 37. ? +−

📖 75

Adhiban, B. – Andreikin, D.

□ 21. ? +−

📖 76

Horvath, A. – Tukhaev, A.

■ 19... ? −+

📖 77

Fressinet, L. – Javakhishvili, L.

☐ 40. ? +−

📖 78

Sadler, M. – Speelman, J.

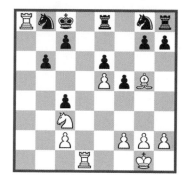

☐ 24. ? +−

📖 79

Guramishvili, S. – Khademalsharieh, S.

☐ 22. ? +−

📖 80 [*]

Matlakov, M. – Smirin, I.

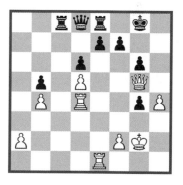

☐ 29. ? +−

Frossinet L. - Javakhishvili, L.

Sadler, M. - Speelman, J.

□ 80 [*]

SOLUTIONS – CHAPTER 5

📖 1

36... ♛b4! (Δ...♛xa3+) **37. ♗a6 ♜xa6 38. ♜d3 ♜h8−+** 0-1 (50) Nataf, I (2526) – Kozul, Z (2611) Istanbul 2000.

📖 2

27. ♛g7+! ♗xg7 28. hxg7+ ♔xh7 29. g8=♛+! 1-0 Vachier Lagrave, M (2493) – David, A (2573) Paris 2004.

Black resigned in view of: 29. g8=♛+ ♜xg8 30. ♜xh4#.

📖 3

29... ♞c3+! 30. bxc3 ♛c2+ 31. ♔a1 ♛xc3+ 32. ♔a2 (32. ♔b1 ♛xb3+ 33. ♔a1 ♛xa3+ 34. ♔b1 ♛b3+ 35. ♔a1 ♜c8−+) **32... ♛c2+ 33. ♔a1 ♛c1+ 34. ♔a2 ♜c8** 0-1 Abergel, T (2499) – Vachier Lagrave, M (2681) Pau 2008.

📖 4

14. ♗g5! ♛xd4 15. ♜e1+ ♗e6

15... ♔f7 16. ♜e7+ ♔g8 17. ♜e8+ ♔g7 *(17... ♔f7 18. ♛xd4 ♞xd4 19. ♜xh8+−)* 18. ♗h6+ ♔f7 19. ♜e7+! ♞xe7 *(19... ♔g8 20. ♛xd4 ♞xd4 21. ♞d5+−)* 20. ♛xd4+−

📖 5

16. ♜xe6+ ♔d7 17. ♜e7+! ♔c8 18. ♜xc7+! ♔b8 (18... ♔xc7 19. ♞b5++−) **19. ♗f4 ♜e8 20. ♜xc6+** 1-0 Seegert, K (2103) – Hartl, D (2249) Fermo 2009.

📖 5

14. e6! fxe6 (14... ♗xe6 15. ♛e5 ♗f6 16. ♛g3++−) **15. ♛g4+ ♔f7 16. ♛g7+** 1-0 Gashimov, V (2740) – Gelfand, B (2756) Lugo 2009.

📖 6

50... ♞h4+!

Black obtains a crushing attack. Instead, the game went 50... ♛f6?↑ 1-0 (85) Jobava, B (2696) – Grischuk, A (2736) Khanty-Mansiysk 2009.

51. gxh4 ♜xf3! 52. ♞xf3 ♛g4+ 53. ♔f1 ♞g3+

Also winning would be: 53... ♜xf3+!? 54. ♞f2 ♞f4 55. ♜h2 ♛g3 *(55... ♞xd3 56. ♛b1 ♞f4−+)* 56. ♛d1□ g5! (Δ...g4) 57. hxg5 hxg5 58. ♜a2 (Δ♛b3+) 58... ♔g7−+.

54. ♔g1 ♞e2+ 55. ♔f1 ♛xf3+ 56. ♞f2 ♛xh1+ 57. ♔xe2 ♛f3+ 58. ♔f1 ♛xd3+ 59. ♛e2 ♛g3 60. ♜d2 (60. ♔e1 ♜f3−+) **60... d3−+**

49... ♗f6!

Instead, the game went 49... ♗f8? 50. ♕e1⇆ 0-1 [58] Carlsen, M [2802] – Radjabov, T [2744] Moscow 2010.

50. ♕e1 [50. g5 hxg5−+] **50... ♗xh4+! 51. ♔xh4 ♕g2−+** [Δ...g5+]

26. d5! [Δ...♕e5+]

26. ♗h6+? would fail: 26... ♔xh6 27. gxh7+ ♔g7 28. h8=♕+ ♖xh8 29. ♘f5+ ♕xf5 30. ♕xf5 ♖c8=.

26... ♘d3□ 27. ♗h6+! ♔xh6 28. gxh7+ ♔g5

28... ♔g7 29. h8=♕+! ♖xh8 [29... ♔xh8 30. ♕h6#] 30. ♘f5+ ♔f8 31. ♕e7+ ♔g8 32. ♕g7#

29. ♕g6+ 1-0 Rapport, R [2543] – Rogic, D [2595] Austria 2010.

Black resigned in view of: 29. ♕g6+ ♔h4 30. h8=♕+ ♖xh8 31. ♘f5+ ♔h3 32. ♕g3#.

18... ♗xb2! 19. ♔xb2 ♖ac8! 20. ♔a1 [20. ♔b1 ♖c2!? 21. ♕xc2 ♖xc2 22. ♔xc2 ♕c6+−+] **20... ♖c2 21. ♕e4 ♕b5 22. ♕d4 ♖xa2+** [22... ♕a5!? 23. a4 ♖d8−+] **23. ♔xa2 ♖c2+ 24. ♔a3 ♕a5+**

25. ♕a4 ♕c5+ 0-1 Negi, P [2596] – Potkin, V [2630] Germany 2011.

White resigned in view of: 25... ♕c5+ 26. ♕b4 ♖c3+ 27. ♔a4 b5+ 28. ♔a5 ♕b6#.

16. h4!! ♗xe4 [16... ♗g6 17. ♕xg6!! fxg6 18. ♗c4+ ♔g8 19. hxg5 gxf6 20. gxf6+−; 16... g4 17. ♕xf5+−] **17. hxg5 ♗xh1 18. ♗d3** [18. fxg7!? ♔xg7 19. ♕h6+ ♔g8 20. ♗d3+−] **18... gxf6** [18... g6 19. ♕h6+−] **19. ♖xh1** [19. ♕h6!? f5 20. ♗xf5+−] **19... ♔f8 20. ♕h6+ ♔e7 21. ♕xf6+ ♔d7 22. ♗f5+ ♖e6 23. ♕xf7++−** 1-0 [30] Negi, P [2631] – Adhiban, B [2551] Germany 2011.

69. ♘e7! a2

69... ♗xe7 70. fxe7 ♕xe7 [70... ♕xf5 71. e8=♕++−] 71. ♕c8++−

70. ♘g6+ ♕xg6 71. ♕xg6 a1=♕+ 72. ♖g1+− 1-0 [75] Kamsky, G [2762] – Karjakin, S [2775] China 2012.

23. e5! ♗xg2 24. ♘b5! ♖cd8

A] 24... ♘d7 25. ♖a8+ ♔xa8 26. ♕a3+ ♔b8 27. ♕a7#

B] 24... dxe5 25. ♕b3+− [Δ♖a8+]

25. ♕c4 d5

25... ♗c6 26. ♕a4 ♔c8 27. ♘a7+ ♔d7 28. ♘xc6 bxc6 29. exd6 ♕e2 *[29... cxd6 30. ♕a7++−]* 30. dxc7++−

26. ♕a4 ♕xa3

26... ♔c8 27. ♘a7+ ♔b8 28. ♘c6+ bxc6 29. ♕a8#

27. ♕xa3+− 1-0 [32] Negi, P [2634] – Portisch, L [2479] Helsingor 2013.

📖 13

29. ♘d5! exd5 30. ♗xf6!+− △♘g7+: 1-0 [34] Kramnik, V [2784] – Fridman, D [2629] Germany 2013.

Black's position is hopeless since 30. ♗xf6 ♘xf6 loses to 31. ♘xf6+ ♔e7 32. ♕e5#.

📖 14

27. ♘g6+! hxg6 28. ♖xh8+ ♗g8 29. ♖eh7!+− △♗h6+: 1-0 Vishnu, P [2523] – Negi, P [2671] Jalgaon 2013.

📖 15

27. h4! h5 [27... h6?! 28. ♗e5+ ♔f5 29. g4#] **28. e4!** It was important to find these first two moves. **28... ♘xe4** [28... dxe4 29. ♗g5+ ♔f5 30. ♖b5++−] **29. fxe4 dxe4 30. g4!** 1-0 Vachier Lagrave, M [2768] – Batchuluun, T [2513] Tromso 2014.

Black resigned in view of: 30. g4 hxg4 31. ♗g5+ ♔f5 32. ♖b5++−.

📖 16

32. ♗f8!

Instead, White played 32. ♖df1? ♖d3 33. ♕xb6 which was also good, but not as strong: ½-½ [47] Grischuk, A [2797] – Karjakin, S [2767] Baku 2014.

32... h5 [32... ♘xf8 33. ♘h6++−; 32... ♗g7 33. ♗xg7+−] **33. ♘h6+ ♔h7 34. ♘f7!** [34. ♖f7+!? ♔g6 35. ♕f2 ♘xf8 36. ♖xd4 ♔xh6 37. ♖xb7+−] **34... ♕xf8 35. ♖xh5+ ♔g6 36. ♘xh8+** [36. ♖xh8+− or 36. ♖f1+− would also win] **36... ♔xh5 37. g4+ ♔h4 38. ♘g6#**

📖 17

28. ♖f4!+− △♖h4: 1-0 Hammer, J [2651] – Burmakin, V [2581] Norway 2015.

Black resigned in view of: 28. ♖f4 ♗xf4 29. ♗d4++−.

📖 18

27... ♖xc4+! The quickest win. **28. dxc4 ♖c3+ 29. bxc3 ♗a3+** 0-1 Motylev, A [2653] – Najer, E [2634] Russia 2015.

White resigned in view of: 29... ♗a3+ 30. ♔d2 ♕xc3+ 31. ♔e2 ♕e3#.

31. ♖e7! ♖xf2 [31... ♖xe7 32. ♗f3#] **32. ♗h3!** The most precise move. **32... h6 33. ♖h7** 1-0 Vachier Lagrave, M (2723) – Hammer, J (2677) Norway 2015.

78... ♕f3!

A) In the game, Black missed that idea and went for a perpetual check: 78... ♕h5+ 79. ♔g2 ♕e2+ 80. ♔h3 ♕h5+ ½-½ Iturrizaga, E (2641) – Zhang, Z (2619) Berlin 2015.

B) 78... ♕f1+ 79. ♔h4 ♕h1+ 80. ♗h3 ♕f3 81. ♗g4 ♕xb3 82. e6=

79. ♕xf7+ ♔h6 80. ♗d5 [80. ♔h2 ♕f1–+] **80... ♕h5+ 81. ♔g2 ♕e2+ 82. ♔h3 ♗g1!** [Δ...♕h2+, ...♕h5#] **83. ♕f8+ ♔h5–+**

19. ♗xh7+!

Instead, the game went 19. b4?± and White lost later on: 0-1 [57] Velikic, A (2322) – Guichard, P (2338) Island 2015.

19... ♔xh7 20. ♕h5+ ♔g8 21. ♗xg7! ♔xg7 22. ♕g5+ ♔f8 23. ♖c4+–

15. ♘g5!

Instead, the game went 15. exf6? ♘xf6± and White lost later on: 0-1 [86] Vishnu, P (2514) – Lenderman, A (2626) England 2015.

15... fxg5 16. ♕h5 16... h6

A) 16... ♖xf4 17. ♕xh7+ ♔f8 18. ♕h8+ ♔f7 19. ♖ae1 ♕d2 20. ♕h5+ ♔f8 21. ♕xg5+–

B) 16... ♖f5 17. ♘xd5!? exd5 18. ♗xf5 ♘f8 19. ♗xh7+ ♘xh7 20. ♕e8+ ♘f8 21. fxg5+–

C) 16... g6 17. ♗xg6 hxg6 18. ♕xg6+ ♔h8 19. ♕h6+ ♔g8 20. ♖f3+–

17. ♕g6 gxf4 18. ♖ae1+–

32. h6+! ♔xh6

32... ♔g8 33. ♕f6+– [Δ♖xc7]

33. ♕f6+–

[Δ♖h1, ♔g1]

33... ♖d7 34. ♖h1 ♘g7 35. ♔g1+ ♘h5 36. ♖xh5+! 1-0 Morozevich, A (2692) – Antipov, M (2569) Russia 2015.

Black resigned in view of: 36. ♖xh5+ ♔xh5 37. ♕h4#.

16. ♘xh6+! gxh6 17. ♗xf7+! ♔xf7 18. ♕h5+ ♔e7

18... ♔g8 19. ♕g6+! ♔h8 20. ♕xe8+−

19. ♘xe4 ♔d8 20. ♘g5!?

A) In the game, White blundered with 20. ♗b6?? ♘xb6 21. ♘f6 ♖xe1+ 22. ♖xe1 ♕g7! 23. ♕e8+ ♔c7 24. axb6+ axb6 25. ♘h5 ♕d4+!?∞ 0-1 [72] Wyss, J [2289] − Kunin, V [2572] Switzerland 2015.

B) However 20. ♗f2!? would also be winning.

20... hxg5 21. ♗b6!+−

23. ♖d1!

Instead, the game went: 23. ♗e3? ♕xc4 24. b3 ♕b4 25. ♖d1 ♗xe6 26. ♘xe6 ♖xe6 27. ♕xf5± ½-½ [42] Adams, M [2744] − Giri, A [2798] Wijk aan Zee 2016.

23... ♕xc5 24. ♖d8+ ♔g7 25. ♗h6+! ♔f6 26. ♗e3! ♕xc4 27. ♕xh7 ♗xe6

27... ♕xe6?! 28. ♖f8++−

28. ♕h8+ ♖g7 29. ♗h6+−

29. ♗g5+!? also wins.

43. f4!

43. ♕f8+ ♔g6 44. f4 gxf4 45. ♕g8+ would transpose as 45... ♕g7 loses to 46. ♕xg7+ ♔xg7 47. ♗d4++−.

43... gxf4 44. ♗c5 ♕g6 45. ♕d8! f6

45... ♕e6 46. ♕h4+ ♔g6 47. ♕h5+ ♔f6 48. ♗d4+ ♔e7 49. ♕c5++−

46. ♗f8+ ♔g5 47. ♕a5+ f5 48. ♕d8+ ♕f6 49. ♗e7 fxg4+ 50. ♔g2+−

1-0 [62] Grandelius, N [2635] − Sundararajan, K [2508] Gibraltar 2016.

24. ♖f6! ♖d8

A) 24... ♔g8 25. ♖xh6 f5 26. ♖d6+−

B) 24... gxf6? 25. ♕xh6+ ♔g8 26. ♘xf6#

25. ♖xh6+ ♔g8 26. ♕g5+− Δ♘f6+: 1-0 Pabalan, R [2089] − Goncalves, J [1984] Gibraltar 2016.

36. f5!! exf5?

Despite a material concession, the least damage would have been: 36... ♖xf5□ 37. ♖c1 ♕xc1+ 38. ♘xc1 ♖f1+

39. ♖g1 ♖cxc1 40. ♕xc1 ♖xc1 41. ♖xc1± keeping some chances.

37. e6+ ♘f6 38. ♘f4 ♗c5 39. ♘h5+ ♔h8 40. ♕h6! ♖c7 41. e7 1-0 Tissir, M [2363] – Cornette, M [2594] Cappelle la Grande 2016.

📖 29

10... ♘xe5! 11. fxe5 ♕h4+ 12. ♔e2 [12. g3? ♕e4+−+] **12... ♗c5! 13. ♗e3** [13. ♘f3? ♕f2+ 14. ♔d3 ♗f5+−+] **13... ♗g4+ 14. ♘f3 d4 15. ♗g1** [15. ♗xd4 ♗xf3+ 16. ♔xf3 ♗xd4 17. g3 ♕d8∓] **15... ♗xf3+** [15... ♘c6−+] **16. ♔xf3 ♘d7 17. g3 ♘xe5+ 18. ♔g2 ♕f6−+** Δ...♖c6: 0-1 [26] Koneru, H [2583] – Ju Wenjun [2558] Teheran 2016.

📖 30

28... ♘f4! 29. exf4 e3 30. fxe3 ♕xf4 31. ♗xf3 [31. ♔f2 ♕h2+ 32. ♔xf3 ♗xd2−+; 31. ♖f2 ♕xe3+−+] **31... ♖xe3+ 32. ♔d1 ♖xf3−+** 0-1 [39] Bat-siashvili, N [2485] – Gunina, V [2496] Tehran 2016.

📖 31

39. ♕d8+! [39. ♖h7? ♖f1 40. ♕xg7+ ♔e7 41. g5□ hxg5+ 42. ♕xg5+ ♔d7∞] **39... ♔g6** [39... ♖e7? 40. ♕b6+ ♖e6 41. ♕xf2++−] **40. g5! ♖f4+** [40... ♖xg2 41. ♖xh6+! gxh6 42. ♕g8#] **41. g4+−** Δ♖xh6+: 1-0 [47] Movsesian, S [2653] – Tomashevsky, E [2728] China 2016.

📖 32

37. ♖xf6! gxf6 38. ♘xf6 ♕c8 39. ♕g6+−

In the [blitz] game, White blundered with 39. d7?? ♕d8−+ 0-1 [49] Socko, M [2448] – Krush, I [2458] China 2016.

📖 33

53. ♕f8+

The game went: 53. ♕xh7+ ♔g5 54. ♕e7+ ♔f5∞ ½-½ [62] Ju Wenjun [2558] – Khotenashvili, B [2502] China 2016.

53... ♔g5 54. ♖f7!+− [Δ♕e7+]

📖 34

37. ♖xd5! exd5 38. ♕xd5 ♕c7 [38... f5 39. ♕d7+ ♔f6 40. ♖d6+ ♕xd6 41. ♕xd6+ ♔g7 42. ♕d2+−] **39. ♕f5 ♖f7** [39... ♕c6 40. ♕h7+ ♔e8 41. ♕xh5+ ♔e7 42. ♗d5+− Δ♕h7+] **40. ♗xf7 ♕e5** [40... ♔xf7? 41. ♕h7++−; 40... ♖e5 41. ♕h7+−] **41. ♖d7+ ♔f8 42. ♖d8+!** 1-0 Karjakin, S [2760] – Caruana, F [2794] Moscow 2016.

Black resigned in view of: 42. ♖d8+ ♔xf7 43. ♕h7+ ♔e6 44. ♕d7#.

📖 35

25. ♕d4!

The only move winning by force. Instead, the game went: 25. ♖h6? ♕e5 26. ♖e3 *(26. ♘f3? ♕f4+!= Oops! This is what I had forgotten in the game!)* 26... ♕d5⇆ 1-0 [80] Edouard, R [2630] – Fridman, D [2642] Germany 2016.

25... ♖fd8 26. ♘xf7! ♖xd6 [26... ♔xf7 27. ♕f6++−] **27. ♘xd6+−**

📖 36

21. ♖g6! ♕c5

A) 21... ♖h6 22. ♘d5+! exd5 23. exd5+ ♘e5 24. ♕f6+ ♔d7 25. ♕e6+ ♔d8 26. ♕e8#

B) 21... ♗h6+ 22. ♖xh6! ♖xh6 23. ♘d5+! exd5 24. exd5+ ♘e5 25. f8=♕++−

22. ♖xe6+! ♔xe6

22... ♔d8 23. ♘d5+−

23. ♘d5+− △♕f5: 1-0 [29] Vallejo Pons, F [2691] – Wynn, Z [2407] Thailand 2016.

📖 37

16. ♘f5+! exf5 17. exf5+ ♔d7 18. ♗e6+ fxe6 19. fxe6+ ♔e7 20. ♕g4 [=20. ♕c2!?] **20... ♗xe6 21. ♕g7+**

♔d8 22. ♕h8+ ♔e7 23. ♕xh7+ ♔d8 24. ♕h8+ ♔d7 25. ♕g7+ ♔d8

White is now crushing Black in several ways. Here some examples...

25... ♔e8 26. ♖c8++−

26. ♕xf6+

26. ♕f8+!? ♔d7 27. ♖xe6 ♖xe6 28. ♖d1++−

26... ♔d7 27. ♕g7+ ♔d8 28. ♕f8+ ♔d7 29. ♖g3

29. ♕c8+ ♔e7 30. ♕xb7+ ♘d7 31. ♕xa8+−

29... ♗c4+ 30. ♔g1+− 1-0 [41] Gagare, S [2491] – Kuzubov, Y [2638] Dubai 2016.

📖 38

15. f4!!

Instead, the game went: 15. ♗xe5? ♘bd7 16. ♗b2 ♗d6 17. ♘de4 ♖e8 18. ♘xf6+ ♘xf6 19. ♕f5± ½-½ [53] Fressinet, L [2692] – Turner, M [2491] England 2016.

15... g6 [15... exf4 16. ♗xf6+−; 15... hxg5 16. hxg5+−] **16. d6!? cxd6 17. ♕xg6+ ♔h8 18. ♗xf7+−**

21. ♘h6+! ♔h8 [21... gxh6 22. ♗b3++−] **22. ♕f7!** [△♕g8+] **22... ♕e6 23. ♗b3 ♕xf7 24. ♘xf7+ ♔g8 25. ♘d6++−** 1-0 [48] Najer, E [2681] – Jakovenko, D [2731] Russia 2016.

45... ♕b1+! 46. ♕f1 [46. ♖f1 ♕xb3 47. ♖xe8 ♕xg3+ 48. ♔g2 ♗xd4+−+] **46... ♖eh8!** 0-1 Turov, M [2630] – Movsesian, S [2688] Wijk aan Zee 2013.

White resigned in view of: 46... ♖eh8 47. ♕xb1 ♖h1+ 48. ♔f2 ♖8h2#.

21. ♔g2! axb6 [21... ♔xb6 22. ♖hd1+−] **22. ♖hd1+−** 1-0 [33] Safarli, E [2664] – Muradli, M [2352] Azerbaijan 2016.

28. ♖xf7+! ♕xf7 [28... ♔xf7 29. ♕h7+ ♔f8 30. ♖g8#] **29. ♕xd6+ ♖e7 30. ♕xb8+ ♕e8 31. ♕d6** 1-0 Nisipeanu, L [2669] – Kozul, Z [2591] Gjakova 2016.

Black resigned in view of: 31. ♕d6 ♕f7 32. ♘e6+ ♔e8 33. ♕d8#.

44. ♕c1+ g5 45. ♕h1! △♔g2/♔g1: 1-0 Bacrot, E [2702] – Kogan, A [2528] Drancy 2016.

26... ♘xf2! 27. ♔xf2 ♕h2+ 28. ♔e3 ♕g2! 29. ♖f1

The game continued: 29. ♕e2 ♖xf3+! 30. ♕xf3 ♗xd4+−+ 0-1 [36] Vachier Lagrave, M [2789] – Anand, V [2770] Leuven 2016.

29... ♘e5!! 30. ♕e2 [30. ♘xe5 ♖xf1−+] **30... ♖xf3+ 31. ♖xf3 ♗xd4+ 32. ♔d2 ♘xf3+−+**

43. ♕e5+! ♔xd7 44. ♗b5+ ♔d8 45. ♕e8+ ♔c7 46. ♕d7+ ♔b8 47. ♕d8+ ♔b7 48. ♗c6+ ♔a6 49. ♕a5# 1-0 Karjakin, S [2774] – Onischuk, V [2613] Kazakhstan 2016.

27. ♗c5+! bxc5 28. ♕xc5+ ♖d6 29. ♕xe5 ♖d1+ 30. ♔g2

The simplest and clearest. Instead, White played the also winning: 30. ♗f1 ♗xf1 [30... ♖xf1+ 31. ♔g2 ♕c6□ 32. ♖b8+ ♔xf7 33. ♕f5+ ♕f6 34. ♕h5+ g6 35. ♕d5+ ♔g7 36. ♖g8+ ♔h6 37. ♕d2+ ♔h5 38. h3 g5 39. g4+ ♔h6 40.

h4+–] **31. ♕c5+** *[31. ♖b8+!? ♔xf7 32.*
♕f5+ ♔e7 33. ♕f8+ ♔e6 34. ♖e8++–]
31... ♔xf7 and now blundered with **32.**
♖f3+?? *[32. ♕h5++– would have won*
the game] **32... ♔e6 33. ♕f5+ ♔d6**
34. ♕f8+ ♔c6?? *[34... ♔e6= would*
have saved the day] **35. ♕e8+ ♔b7**
36. ♕xa4 1-0 Kramnik, V [2812] – Aronian, L [2792] Leuven 2016.

30... ♗f1+ 31. ♔f3! ♗xh3 32. ♖b8+
♔xf7 33. ♕h5++–

📖 47

25. ♘f6+! gxf6 26. exf6 ♖e4□ [26...
♖e6 will transpose to the game.] **27.**
♕f5! ♖e6 [27... ♕a4 28. ♖xd5 cxd5
29. ♕g5+ ♔f8 30. ♕g7+ ♔e8 31.
♕g8+ ♔d7 32. ♕xf7+ ♔d6 33. ♕c7+
♔e6 34. ♕e7+ ♔f5 35. ♕xd8+–] **28.**
b4! The most precise, now or later.
28... ♕b6 29. ♕g5+ ♔f8 30. ♕g7+
♔e8 31. ♖e1 [31. ♕g8+ ♔d7 32. ♕xf7+
♔d6 33. ♕g7 was even stronger] **31...**
♖xe1+ [31... ♘f6 32. ♖xe6+ fxe6 33.
♕xf6+–] **32. ♖xe1+ ♔d7 33. ♕xf7+**
♔c8 34. ♕e6+ ♔b8 35. f7 ♕c7 36.
♕e8+– 1-0 Donchenko, A [2583] –
Hacker, J [2275] Warsaw 2016.

📖 48

24. ♘xg7!

Instead, the game went: 24. ♗e3
♕c6⇆ 1-0 [31] Bilguun, S [2419] – Dragun, K [2623] Warsaw 2016.

24... ♔xg7 25. ♘xf6 ♖xf6 [25... ♗xf6
26. ♕h5+–] **26. ♗xf6+ ♗xf6 27.**
♕h5 ♕c6 [27... ♖h8 28. ♖xe5+–] **28.**
♕xh7+ ♔f8 29. ♖f3!? ♕e6 [29... e4
30. ♖g3+–] **30. ♖f2+–** [△♖ef1]

📖 49

23... ♕c6! 24. ♘xf8 ♕b5+ 25. ♖d3
♖c3 26. ♗xf7+ [26. ♖hd1 b1=♕–+]
26... ♔xf8 0-1 Fedorchuk, S [2624] –
Moussard, J [2521] Paris 2016.

📖 50

27... e3!

Instead, the game went: 27... ♘xf4?
28. ♕g3⇆ 1-0 [43] Sargissian, G
[2679] – Khademalsharieh, S [2445]
Iran 2016.

28. fxe3

A] 28. ♖d3 ♖de8 29. ♗g2 *[29. fxe3*
♕h6 30. ♗g2 ♘xf4! 31. ♘xf4 ♗xg2+
32. ♔xg2 ♖g8+–+] 29... ♖xf4! 30.
♘xf4 ♕xf4 31. ♖c2 ♕f5–+

B] 28. ♗g2 ♖xf4! 29. ♘xf4 ♕xf4 30.
♖c2 ♕g4 31. f3 ♖f8 32. ♖d3 ♕f5 with
a crushing attack, for example: 33.
♖e2 ♘f4 34. ♖dxe3 ♗d5! 35. ♕d1
♗c4–+

28... ♖de8! 29. ♖d3 [29. ♔f2 ♕h6
30. ♖h1 ♕h4+ 31. ♘g3 ♘xf4–+] **29...**
♕h6–+

32... ♘xf2! 33. ♔xf2 ♕h2 34. ♕f3

The game continued: 34. ♖e1 ♖f6+ 35. ♔e2 ♖e8+ 0-1 [35] Zanan, E [2450] – Laznicka, V [2654] Czech Republic 2016 *[White resigned in view of: 35... ♖e8+ 36. ♔d1 ♖xe1+ 37. ♔xe1 ♕g1+–+].*

34... ♖e3!

The strongest. The most important was to find the first two moves of the solution, and to understand the evaluation of the position.

Black is winning, here some examples:

35. ♕g4 ♖de8 Δ...♖3e4 [35... f5!? 36. ♕h5 ♔g7 is also very strong] **36. ♖xd4** [36. ♖ac1 ♖3e4–+] **36... ♕e5** [36... f5 37. ♕d1 g4 38. hxg4 ♕h4+ 39. ♔f1 ♕h1+ 40. ♔f2 ♖e2+ 41. ♕xe2 ♖xe2+ 42. ♔xe2 ♕xa1 should also win] **37. ♔g1** [37. ♖ad1 f5 38. ♕h5 ♕g3+ 39. ♔f1 ♖e1+ 40. ♖xe1 ♖xe1#; 37. ♖dd1 ♖e4 38. ♕h5 ♖h4 39. ♕f3 ♖f4–+] **37... f5 38. ♕d1 ♖e1+ 39. ♕xe1 ♕xd4+–+**

21. ♖d5! exd5 22. ♗xd5+ ♔f8 23. ♕e6 ♔e8 24. ♗xe5 ♔d8 [24... ♖d8 25. ♕g8+ ♔d7 26. ♗e6++–] **25. c4+–** 1-0 [38] Korobov, A [2656] – Sutovsky, E [2622] Russia 2016.

14. ♘e4! dxe5 [14... ♗xe1 15. ♘xf6+ gxf6 16. ♗xf6+–] **15. ♘xf6+ gxf6 16. ♖xe5!** [16. ♖e3!? is not as strong but also winning.] **16... ♖xe5 17. ♗h7+ ♔xh7 18. ♕xd8+–** 1-0 [20] Kovchan, A [2576] – Nezad, H [2419] Biel 2016.

31... e3! 32. ♖xe3 [32. ♗xe3 ♕g3–+] **32... ♗xe3 33. ♗xe3 ♕g3–+** 0-1 [37] Stephan, V [2380] – Lagarde, M [2572] Agen 2016.

21... ♗xd4!!

Instead, the game went: 21... ♘b4? 22. ♖d1 ♗b7⩲ 0-1 [35] Stupak, K [2561] – Bok, B [2592] Baku 2016.

22. ♕xd4

22. ♘xd4 ♘b4!? *[22... ♕e5+ 23. ♔d2 ♘f6–+]* 23. ♕xb4 ♖xd4 24. ♕b5 ♗a6! 25. ♕xa6 ♕e5+ 26. ♔f3 ♕e4#

22... ♘f4+! 23. ♕xf4 ♕xb2+ 24. ♘d2 ♗a6+ 25. ♔f3 ♗b7+ 26. ♔e2 ♕xa1 27. f3 [27. ♕xh6 ♕e5+ 28. ♔d1 ♗xh1–+] **27... ♕b2–+** Δ...♗a6+

33... ♖f3! 34. e6

34. ♕d5 ♖g3+ 35. fxg3 ♕xg3+ 36. ♔h1 ♖f1+–+

34... ♖g3+! 35. fxg3 ♕f1+!

35... ♕xg3+? 36. ♔h1 ♖f1+ 37. ♔g1 ♕xh3+ 38. ♖h2 ♕f3+ 39. ♔g2=

36. ♔h2 ♗xg3+ 0-1 Wang, Y [2737] – Mareco, S [2606] Baku 2016.

White resigned in view of: 36... ♗xg3+ 37. ♔xg3 ♖f3+ 38. ♔h4 ♕xh3+ 39. ♔g5 ♕h6#.

34. f6!

Instead, the game went: 34. ♗xe7? exf4 35. ♗xf8 ♗xd4 36. ♕g4 *[Just for the pleasure of seeing a beautiful line – the engine now gives 36. f6 as a forced draw: 36... ♗xf6 37. ♕d7 ♕xe3+ 38. ♔h1 ♕d4 39. ♕e8 ♔xh7 40. ♗d6!! avoiding 40... ♕e5, and Black cannot avoid a perpetual check with ♕h5-♕e8 in a proper way!]* 36... ♖c7–+ 0-1 [63] Li, C [2746] – Short,N [2666] Baku 2016.

34... gxf6 [34... ♖xf6 35. ♖xf6 gxf6 36. ♗xe4 ♗xe4 37. ♗xf6+ ♕xf6 38. ♖g8#] **35. ♗xe4! ♗xe4 36. ♗xf6+! ♖xf6 37. ♖g8#**

31. ♘h5+! gxh5 [31... ♔h8 32. ♕xf8+ ♖xf8 33. ♖xf8#] **32. ♗h6+! ♔xh6** [32... ♔g8 33. ♕xf8+ ♖xf8 34. ♖xf8#] **33. ♕f6#** 1-0 Hou Yifan [2649] – Jackson, J [2311] England 2016.

21. ♘xf7!! ♔xf7 22. ♗xf6! gxf6 23. ♘e5+ ♔g7 24. ♕g4+ 1-0 Zeller, F [2395] – Georgiadis, N [2483] SUI 2016.

After 24. ♕g4+ ♔f8 25. ♕xb4+ ♔g8 White can win several ways, e.g. 26. ♕g4+ ♔f8 27. ♕f4 ♔g7 28. ♘xd7 ♖xd7 29. ♖xd7+ ♕xd7 30. ♕xb8+–

29. ♖xf6! ♗xf6 30. ♘h5! gxh5 31. ♕xf6+ ♔g8 32. ♖e3+– 1-0 [39] Hou Yifan [2649] – Short, N [2670] Hoogeveen 2016.

30. ♘xf7+! ♖xf7 31. ♖xe6 ♕xb5 32. ♖h6+ 1-0 Caruana, F [2823] – Nakamura, H [2779] London 2016.

Black resigned in view of: 32. ♖h6+ ♔g8 33. ♖g1+ ♔f8 *[33... ♖g7 34. ♗e6+ ♔f8 35. ♖h8+ ♔e7 36. ♖xg7+ ♔xe6 37. ♖h6#]* 34. ♖h8+ ♔e7 35. ♖xb8 ♕xb8 36. ♗c5+ ♔f6 *[36... ♔d8 37. ♖g8++–]* 37. ♖g6#.

📖 62

26. ♘xf7+! ♔xf7 27. e6 ♗xe6 [27...
♘xf6 28. exf7+−] **28. ♖xe6 ♖xe6
29. ♖xe6 ♕a2** [29... ♕c1+ 30. ♖e1+−]
**30. ♘xd7 ♔xd7 31. ♖xe7+! ♔xe7 32.
♕c7+ ♔e6 33. ♕c6+ ♔e7 34. ♕xc5+
♔e6 35. ♕c6+ ♔e7 36. ♕b7+** 1-0 Wei
Yi [2707] − Rapport, R [2717] Yancheng
2016

Black resigned in view of: 36. ♕b7+
♔e6 37. ♗xh8+−.

📖 63

18. ♘xe6! fxe6 19. ♖hf1! ♔d8 [19... h6
20. ♕d6+ ♔d8 21. ♖f7 ♖a7 22. ♕c5
♕b8 23. ♕c6+−] **20. ♖f7 ♖a7 21. ♕f2!
♔c8 22. ♖dxd7 ♕xd7 23. ♕xa7+−** 1-0
[27] Van Foreest, J [2605] − Liang, A
[2495] Sitges 2016.

📖 64

17. ♖xf7! ♖xf7

17... ♘xc5 18. ♖d7+ ♔h8 19. ♖xd8 ♖xd8
20. ♗d5+− 1-0 [49] Svane, R [2555] −
Mamedov, R [2688] Doha 2016.

**18. ♗xf7+ ♔xf7 19. ♕b3+ ♔e7 20.
e5!!**

The strongest move, although 20.
♘e6 ♕g8 21. ♕a3 ♔f7 22. ♖c7 is also
crushing.

After the killer 20.e5 White is winning,
here some examples:

📖 65

20... h6 [20... ♘xe5 21. ♗g5+ ♗f6 22.
♖xe5++−; 20... ♘xc5 21. ♘c6+! bxc6
22. ♗xc5++−] **21. ♕e6+ ♔f8 22. ♖c2
♕e7 23. ♗xh6!?** [23. ♖f2+ ♘f6 24.
♕d5+−; 23. ♕xg6 ♘xe5 24. ♖xc8+
♖xc8 25. ♕f5++−] **23... ♕xe6 24.
♘xe6+ ♔f7 25. ♘xg7 ♘xe5 26. ♖c7+
♗d7 27. ♗f4+−**

📖 65

**20. ♕xg5+ ♔f7 21. ♕xh5+!! ♗xh5
22. ♗xh5+ ♔g8 23. ♖g1+ ♘g7 24.
♖xg7+ ♔h8 25. ♖xe7+ ♔f6 26. ♗xf6+
♔g8 27. ♖g7+ ♔f8 28. ♖xh7 ♕f5 29.
♖h8#** 1-0 Radjabov, T [2710] − Bortnyk, O [2581] Doha 2016.

📖 66

35. ♗h5! ♕g8 [35... ♕xh5 36. ♕f8+
♔g6 37. ♕e8+ ♔h6 38. ♗f8+ ♔g7 39.
♗xg7+ ♔xg7 40. ♕xh5+−] **36. ♕c7+**
[36. ♕a7+ ♔h6 37. ♕xa6 ♔xh5 38.
♕xc6+−] **36... ♔h6 37. ♕xc6 ♔xh5
38. ♕xa6+−** 1-0 [48] Mamedyarov, S
[2768] − Korobov, A [2692] Doha 2016.

📖 67

**18. ♘d5! exd5 19. ♖xf7! ♔xf7 20.
♗xd5+ ♔e8** [20... ♔f8 21. ♕h5+−] **
21. ♕h5+ ♔d8 22. ♘e6+ ♗xe6 23.
♗xe6+ ♗d6 24. ♖xd6+ ♕xd6 25.
exd6 ♖f8 26. ♕a5+** 1-0 Jobava, B
[2702] − Atabayev, M [2492] Doha
2016.

📖 68

22. ♖xe6! ♖xe6 23. ♗f7++– 1-0 [31] Salem, A (2656) – Ivanchuk, V (2747) Doha 2016.

📖 69

19. g5! hxg5 20. h6! g6

20... gxf4 21. ♗h7+ *[21. hxg7!? also wins]* 21... ♚h8 22. hxg7+ ♚xg7 23. ♖dg1+ ♗g5 24. ♖h5+–

21. ♗xd6 ♗xd6 22. ♗xg6 ♕f6 23. ♗f5+– 1-0 [35] Dubov, D (2660) – Dominguez Perez, L (2739) Doha 2016.

📖 70

46. ♖e6! ♖xe6 [46... ♖dd7 47. ♖e7 ♕d5 48. ♕xd7 ♕xd7 49. ♖xd7 ♖xd7 50. ♖e7+ ♖xe7 51. fxe7+–] **47. ♕xf7+** 1-0 Chu Wei Chao (2289) – Bellahcene, B (2493) Basel 2017.

📖 71

17. ♘f6+ ♚h8 18. ♘h5 ♖g8 19. ♖d8! 1-0 Safarli, E (2686) – Donchenko, A (2559) Basel 2017.

📖 72

31... ♕a1+ 32. ♚c2 ♖d2+! 33. ♚xd2 ♕xb2+ 34. ♚e3 ♖e8+ 35. ♚e4 ♕xc3+ 36. ♚f2 ♕c2+ 37. ♖e2 ♗c5+–+ 0-1

Forcen Esteban, D (2541) – Vazquez Igarza, R (2572) Roquetas de Mar 2017.

📖 73

40. ♘h4+! ♚g5 [40... ♚e6 41. ♘f4+ ♚f7 42. ♖g1+–] **41. ♖g6+! ♚xh4** [41... ♚h5 42. ♘f4++–] **42. ♖h1+ ♗h3 43. ♖g3** 1-0 Harikrishna, P (2766) – Adhiban, B (2653) Wijk aan Zee 2017.

📖 74

37. e5!

The game went 37. ♖d2? ♖e8 38. ♕h6+? ♚e7 39. e5 ♖g8! 40. ♕xd6+ ♕xd6 41. exd6+ ½-½ Giri, A (2773) – Andreikin, D (2736) Wijk aan Zee 2017.

37... d5

A) 37... ♕d8 38. ♕g7+ ♚e8 39. ♕g8+ ♚e7 40. exd6+ ♕xd6 41. ♖e2++–

B) 37... dxe5 38. ♕h8+ ♚e7 39. ♕xe5+ ♚f8 40. ♕g7+ ♚e7 41. ♖e2++–

38. e6! ♕xe6 [38... ♖b7 39. e7+! ♖xe7 40. ♕h8#] **39. ♕h8++–**

📖 75

21. ♖xf5! ♘xf5 22. ♖xf5 ♕d4+ [22... ♗xf5 23. ♘xf5 gxf5 24. ♘f6++–; 22... gxf5 23. ♘f6++–] **23. ♖f2+–** 1-0 [46] Adhiban, B (2653) – Andreikin, D (2736) Wijk aan Zee 2017.

📖 76

19... ♘b3+! 20. axb3 a4 21. ♗d3

The gamed ended with: 21. ♘c7 a3 0-1
Horvath, A (2499) – Tukhaev, A (2516)
Chennai 2017.

**21... axb3+ 22. ♗a5 ♛xd1+! 23.
♛xd1 ♖xa5+ 24. ♔b1 ♖fa8 25. ♛xb3
♘d2+–+**

📖 77

40. ♖g6! 1-0 Fressinet, L (2660) – Javakhishvili, L (2455) Gibraltar 2017.

Black resigned in view of: 40. ♖g6
fxg6 41. ♖xh6+ gxh6 42. ♛xh6#.

📖 78

24. ♘b5! (Δ♖a7) 24... ♖e7

A) 24... ♔b7 25. ♖a7+ ♔c6 26. ♘xc7+–

B) 24... ♘e7 25. ♖a7 ♘d5 26. ♖xd5
exd5 27. ♖xc7#

25. ♖xb8+ 1-0 Sadler, M (2670) –
Speelman, J (2526) Reading 2017.

Black resigned in view of: 25. ♖xb8+
♔xb8 26. ♖d8+ ♔b7 27. ♗xe7+–.

📖 79

22. ♛h6! (Δ♘e7+)

≤ 22. ♗e2± was played in the game,
and White won later on anyway: 1-0
(31) Guramishvili, S (2357) – Khademalsharieh, S (2452) Tehran 2017.

22... gxf5

22... f6 23. ♘e7+ ♔f7 24. ♛xh7++–

23. ♗c2!?

Any bishop move wins! Δ♖g3

23... f6 24. ♖g3+ ♔f7 25. ♛xh7++–

📖 80

29. ♖e6! (Δ♖xg6+)

Instead, the game went: 29. ♖xg4
♖c4 30. h5 ♖xg4+ 31. ♛xg4 ♛c8⇆
½-½ (38) Matlakov, M (2701) – Smirin, I
(2670) Moscow 2017.

29... ♖c4□ (29... ♔g7 30. ♖xg4+–;
29... ♔h7 30. h5+–] **30. ♖xg6+! fxg6
31. ♛xg6+ ♔f8 32. ♛f5+ ♔g7 33.
♛xg4+ ♔h8** [=33... ♔h6 34. ♛g5+
♔h7 35. ♛h5++–; 33... ♔f6 34. ♛g5+
♔f7 35. ♛f5+ ♔g7 36. ♖d3+–] **34.
♛h5+ ♔g7 35. ♖d3! ♖g8 36. ♖g3+
♔f6 37. ♛h6+ ♔e5** [37... ♔f7 38.
♛h7++–] **38. ♛e6+ ♔d4 39. ♖xg8+–**

Chapter 6

Find the stunning winning move!

This chapter contains a selection of difficult positions where you must find a spectacular or unusual winning move.

In most of the exercises, the "hidden" winning move is made immediately. In a few examples, however, it is on move 2, the first move being merely preparatory.

You must focus on the following issues: seriously disrupting your opponent's coordination, preventing problems (prophylaxis: finding your opponent's ideal move should lead you to the solution!), bringing an extra piece into the action, destroying the enemy king.

You may wish to use the help page which you will find at page 151. Don't give up!

📖 1

Jobava, B. – Mamedov, R.

■ 27... ? −+

📖 2

Negi, P. – Hou Yifan

□ 35. ? +−

📖 3

Gunina, V. – Sutovsky, E.

□ 32. ? +−

📖 4

Harikrishna, P. – Movsesian, S.

□ 43. ? +−

5

Caruana, F. – So, W.

■ 37... ? −+

 6

Nepomniachtchi, I. – Sjugirov, S.

□ 10. ? ±

 **7**

Ipatov, A. – Brkic, A.

□ 27. ? +−

📖 **8**

Caruana, F. – Nakamura, H.

□ 45. ? +−

9

Firouzja, A. – Dreev, A.

■ 27... ? −+

10

Jakovenko, D. – Bologan, V.

□ 15. ? +−

11

Bauer, C. – Feller, S.

□ 24. ? +−

12

Durarbayli, V. – Ivanisevic, I.

■ 31... ? −+

13

Lu, S. – Bok, B.

■ 33... ? −+
The most difficult exercise,
in my opinion!

 14

Riff, J. – Gulamali, K.

□ 29. ? +−

15

Svidler, P. – Short, N.

□ 28. ? +−

16

Pert, N. – Batchelor, P.

□ 20. ? +−

HELP PAGE!

Subjects of the exercises of the sixth chapter…

📖 1:   serious disrupting of your opponent's coordination.
📖 2:   prophylaxis & bring an extra piece into the action!
📖 3:   serious disrupting of your opponent's coordination.
📖 4:   bring an extra piece into the action!
📖 5:   serious disrupting of your opponent's coordination.
📖 6:   bring an extra piece into the action!
📖 7:   bring an extra soldier into the action!
📖 8:   prophylaxis (solve the defensive problem before going for an attack!).
📖 9:   serious disrupting of your opponent's coordination.
📖 10: destruction of the opponent's King!
📖 11: serious disrupting of your opponent's coordination.
📖 12: prophylaxis & serious disrupting of your opponent's coordination.
📖 13: 100% prophylaxis. Think of White's next move!
📖 14: bring an extra piece into the action & destruction of the opponent's King.
📖 15: serious disrupting of your opponent's coordination & destruction of the opponent's King.
📖 16: bring an extra piece into the action & destruction of the opponent's King.

SOLUTIONS – CHAPTER 6

📖 1

27... ♗a4!! 28. ♕d3 [28. ♕xa4 ♗xc3 29. ♕xb4 ♗xb4–+; 28. ♘xa4 ♕xe1+–+] **28... ♘f2! 29. ♕xe3** [29. ♗xf2 ♖xf2–+] **29... ♖ae8** [The game move is stronger, but 29... ♘xh3 also wins.] **30. ♕d2 ♘xh3–+** 0-1 [32] Jobava, B [2721] – Mamedov, R [2628] Tbilisi 2012.

📖 2

35. ♗e3!!

Anticipating ...♔h7 while threatening 36. ♗h6.

Instead, the game went: 35. ♕h6+? ♖h7 36. ♕f6+ ♖hg7 37. d6? ♔h7⇆ 0-1 [39] Negi, P [2664] – Hou Yifan [2683] Saint Louis USA 2015.

35... ♕xe3 [35... ♔h7? 36. ♕h6#] **36. ♕xh4+ ♖h7 37. ♕f6+ ♖hg7** [37... ♖gg7 38. ♕d8++–] **38. ♖h1++–**

📖 3

32. ♖b8+!

Instead, the game went: 32. ♘f6+? ♔g7 33. ♖7b2 ♖axb2 34. ♖xb2 ♖xc7 35. ♘xd5= ½-½ [36] Gunina, V [2496] – Sutovsky, E [2647] Gibraltar 2016.

32... ♔g7 33. ♖a1!! ♖d2+ [33... ♖ab2 34. ♖xb2 ♖xb2 35. ♖a6 ♘c8 36. ♖a8+–] **34. ♔e1 ♖e2+** [34... ♖ac2 35. c8=♕ ♘xc8 36. ♖xc8+–] **35. ♔f1 ♖xh2 36. ♖xa2 ♖xa2 37. ♖d8+–**

📖 4

43. ♘bc8!! [Δ♘e7/♖xg6+]

Instead, the game went: 43. ♘f5+? ♔f7 44. ♖d6 ♖xd6? [44... gxf5! 45. ♘d7□ ♔e7□ 46. ♖xc6 bxc6∞] 45. ♘xd6+ ♔g7 46. ♘f5+ ♔f7 47. ♖xg6! ♕xb6 48. ♖g7+! ♔f8 49. ♕d7+– 1-0 [62] Harikrishna, P [2753] – Movsesian, S [2653] China 2016.

43... ♖xc8 [43... ♗g5 44. ♕b3+–] **44. ♘xc8 ♖xc8 45. ♖d7++–** White wins, e.g. **45... ♔f8** [45... ♔h8 46. ♖h1+ ♔g8 47. ♖h8+! ♔xh8 48. ♕h1++–] **46. ♖h1 ♔e8 47. ♖d6 ♕c4 48. ♖h8+ ♘f8 49. ♖xf6+–**

📖 5

37... ♘f3+!!

37... ♘e6? 38. ♖xe6 fxe6 39. ♕xe6+ ♔f8 40. ♕f6+= ½-½ [42] Caruana, F [2795] – So, Wesley [2773] USA 2016.

38. ♕xf3 ♕g7–+

10. ♗xh7+! ♔xh7 11. h4! Bringing the h1-Rook in! **11... ♗d2+** [11... ♗xh4 12. ♕d3+ ♔g8 13. ♖xh4 f5 14. g3±] **12. ♕xd2 ♖e8+ 13. ♔f1 ♗xf3 14. ♕d3+ ♔g8 15. ♕xf3±** 1-0 [32] Nepomniachtchi, I [2703] – Sjugirov, S [2674] Russia 2016.

27. h4!! [27. f6?? ♕g4∓; 27. h3? ♕e8! 28. f6 ♕g8⇆; 27. g4? ♕d8! 28. ♖h3 ♕d5+=] **27... ♕e8** [27... c3 28. h5 ♕d8 29. ♖d7!! ♕xd7 30. ♕f6+ ♔g8 31. h6 ♕d2+ 32. ♔f2+−; 27... ♕d8 28. f6+−] **28. h5** 1-0 Ipatov, A [2648] – Brkic, A [2584] Gjakova 2016.

45. f4!!

Instead, the game went: 45. ♕c4+? ♔e7 46. ♖d2 ♕e5+⇆ ½-½ [69] Caruana, F [2804] – Nakamura, H [2787] Belgium 2016.

45... exf3 46. ♖h8 f2 [46... ♖e7 47. ♖xh7+ ♔e8 48. ♕c6+ ♔f8 49. ♕a8+ ♖e8 50. ♖h8+ ♔g7 51. ♕xe8 ♕c2+ 52. ♔g3 ♕g2+ 53. ♔f4+−] **47. ♖xh7+ ♔e6** [47... ♔e8 48. ♖xb7+−] **48. ♕c6+ ♔e5 49. ♕xb7 f1=♕ 50. ♖e7+ ♔d6 51. ♕c7+ ♔d5 52. e4+ ♔d4** [52... ♕xe4 53. ♖d7+ ♔e6 54. ♕d6+ ♔f5 55. ♖f7+ ♔g4 66. ♕g3+ ♔h5 67. ♖h7#] **53. ♕d6+ ♔c4 54. exf5 ♕f2+ 55. ♔h3 ♕f1+** [55... ♕f3+ 56. ♔g3+−] **56. ♔g4+−**

27... ♗d2!! 28. ♘xd2 [28. ♕xd2 ♕xe4−+; 28. ♖xd2 ♕xc1+ 29. ♖xc1 ♖xc1#] **28... ♕c2+ 29. ♔a1 ♖b5! 30. b3** [30. ♕e4 ♖xb2−+] **30... ♖a5 31. a4 ♘b4** 0-1 Firouzja, A [2481] – Dreev, A [2664] Iran 2016.

15. ♗g5! ♕d6 [15... ♗xg5 16. ♗b5 ♕e6 17. ♖e1+−; 15... c4 16. ♗e4 ♕c5 17. ♗xe7 ♔xe7 18. ♕e2 ♔f6 19. ♘d4!+− Δ♕f3+; 15... f6 16. ♗g6++−] **16. ♗b5 ♕c7** [16... ♕g6 17. ♖xd8+ ♔xd8 18. ♖d1+ ♔c8 19. ♕xg6 hxg6 20. ♗xc6 ♗xc6 21. ♗xe7+−] **17. ♖xd8+ ♔xd8 18. ♖d1+ ♔e8** [18... ♔c8 19. ♕f5+ ♔b8 20. ♗f4+−] **19. ♕e4 f6 20. ♗f4 ♕c8 21. ♖d6+−** 1-0 Jakovenko, D [2712] – Bologan, V [2654] Russia 2016.

24. ♗b7!! ♗xb7 25. ♘e6 ♕b8 [25... ♕e7 26. ♘xf8+ ♕xf8 27. ♖xa7+−] **26. ♗xa7 ♖xa7 27. ♘xf8+ ♔g8 28. ♘e6+−** 1-0 [30] Bauer, C [2620] – Feller, S [2602] Agen 2016.

31... ♗f8!!

Instead, the game went: 31... ♖xd1+? 32. ♖xd1 ♕h5 33. ♗b3 ♖g8 34. ♗f4± 1-0 [67] Durarbayli, V [2612] – Ivanisevic, I [2650] Baku 2016.

32. ♗xf8 ♖8b2 33. ♕xb2 ♖xb2 34. ♖7d2□ ♖xd2 35. ♖xd2 ♕a5 36. ♖d1 ♔g8–+

📖 13

33... h5!!

Preventing the crucial ♕g4-♕c4. Now he simply does not have a move.

A) Instead, Black played 33... ♖c8? and later lost: 34. ♕g4 ♖f8 35. ♕c4+– 1-0 (52) Lu Shanglei [2612] – Bok, B [2608] Wijk aan Zee 2017.

B) The brutal 33... e4? also fails: 34. ♕g4 *(34. ♕g3 ♕e2+ 35. ♔a3 ♘d3 36. ♗d4 is also playable)* 34... h5 35. ♕g5 ♕e2+ 36. ♔a3 ♘d4 37. ♗d2 and White is fine!

34. h4□ *(Δ...♖c8, ♕h3)*

A) 34. ♕h1 ♕e2+ 35. ♔c3 ♘d3–+;

B) 34. ♖b6 ♘e4 *(34... ♖c8!?–+)* 35. ♕h1 *(35. ♖c6 ♖b8–+)* 35... ♕e2+ 36. ♔a3 ♘c3 37. ♕a1 ♕c2–+.

34... ♖e8!? White is in zugzwang! E.g. **35. ♖b5** (35. a5 ♖a8–+; 35. ♔a3 ♕f1 36. ♔a2 ♘d3 37. ♖c4 e4 38. ♖xe4 ♖xe4 39. ♕xe4 ♕e2+–+) **35... ♖c8 36. ♖b4** (36. ♕h3?! ♘xa4+–+) **36... ♘a6 37. ♖b6 ♕c3+ 38. ♔a2 ♘b4+–+**

📖 14

29. ♗f4! (29. ♗h2?? ♕f6 30. g4+ ♔h4

31. ♔g2 ♗f1+–+) **29... ♖xe5**

After 29... ♕f6? the game soon ended: 30. g4+ ♔h4 31. ♔h2! 1-0 Riff, J [2468] – Gulamali, K [2341] Gibraltar 2017.

30. ♗xe5 ♖e8 (30... f6 31. g4+ ♔h4 32. ♕g6!+–) **31. ♗f4!!** (Δg4, ♔h2) **31... ♕e1+** (31... ♕e6 32. g4+ ♔h4 33. ♗xg5+ hxg5 34. ♕h7++–; 31... ♕e4 32. ♕xf7++–) **32. ♔h2 ♕xf2 33. ♕xf7+ ♔h4 34. ♗xg5++–**

📖 15

28. ♕e6+

Instead, the game went 28. ♗b5? And after 28... ♘e5 Black was fine: 29. ♗d4 ♗g3 30. ♗xe5 ½-½ Svidler, P [2748] – Short, N [2675] Gibraltar 2017.

28... ♔g7 29. ♗b5!! ♖xb5 30. ♗f8+! ♔xf8 31. ♕f6+ ♕f7 (31... ♔g8 32. ♖e8#) **32. ♕h8+ ♕g8 33. ♖f1++–**

📖 16

20. ♗b5!! fxe5 21. ♖d7 ♕b8 (21... ♕c8 22. ♕xe5 ♖f7 23. ♕xe6 ♕e8 24. ♗c4+–) **22. hxg6 ♖f5**

22... hxg6 was played but wasn't a better defence: 23. ♕g4 ♖f6 24. ♕h3 ♖f7 25. ♕xe6 1-0 Pert, N [2566] – Batchelor, P [2361] Reading 2017.

23. ♕g4!? (23. ♖xh7+–) **23... h5 24. ♕xf5!! exf5 25. ♗c4+ ♔f8 26. g7+ ♔e8 27. ♗e6+–**

Chapter 7

Play the killer positional move!

In this chapter, you must find strong positional moves. The solution is always concrete and the evaluation of the position which will result should be very helpful.

A good positional move does not mean there are no tactics involved! On the contrary, this series of exercises is intended to help you to intelligently mix tactics and strategy.

The difficulty of these exercises ranges from medium to difficult, the most challenging ones being marked with an asterisk.

📖 1

Edouard, R. – Ekstroem, R.

■ 21... ? ∓

📖 2

Kramnik, V. – Vitiugov, N.

□ 45. ? +−

📖 3 [*]

Van Kampen, R. – Adams, M.

□ 20. ? ±

📖 4 [*]

Kovalyov, A. – Van Kampen, R.

■ 17... ? =

5

Mamedyarov, S. – Ragger, M.

☐ 18. ? ±

 6

Smirin, I. - Radjabov, T.

■ 29... ? −+

 7 [*]

Vachier Lagrave, M. – Studer, N.

☐ 12. ? ±

 8

Harikrishna, P. – Grandelius, N.

☐ 40. ? +−

📖 9

Maze, S. – Hamdouchi, H.

□ 32. ? ±/+−

📖 10

Krasenkow, M. – Hammer, J.

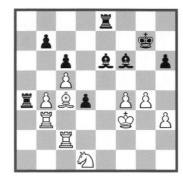

■ 31... ? ∓/−+

📖 11

Khademalsharieh, S. – Harika, D.

□ 40. ? +−

📖 12

Kramnik, V. – Giri, A.

□ 34. ? +−

13 (*)

Feller, S. – Miron, L.

□ 30. ? +−

 14

Trent, L. – Efimenko, Z.

■ 28... ? ∓

 15

Hector, J. – Bacrot, E.

■ 27... ? ∓

 16 (*)

Baskin, R. – Neef, M.

□ 20. ? +−

📖 17

Demuth, A. – Bluebaum, M.

■ 26... ? ∓

📖 18

Melkumyan, H. – Veleski, R.

□ 66. ? +−

📖 19

Salgado Lopez, I. – Solodovnichenko, Y.

□ 14. ? ±

📖 20

Caruana, F. – Topalov, V.

□ 19. ? +−

21

Lalith, B – Edouard, R.

■ 16. ? ∓

 22 [*]

Bogner, S. – Georgiadis, N.

□ 14. ? ±

📖 23 [*]

Dreev, A. – Maghsoodloo, P.

□ 40. ? ±

📖 24

Rasmussen, A. – Fressinet, L.

□ 37. ? +−

📖 25

Artemiev, V. – Idani, P.

■ 19… ? ∓

📖 26

Moncamp, G. – Lagarde, M.

■ 13… ? ∓

📖 27

Naiditsch, A. – Henriquez Villagra, C.

■ 25… ? ∓

📖 28

Vocaturo, D. – Shvayger, Y.

■ 16… ? ∞

📖 29

Edouard, R. – Vega Gutierrez, S.

□ 27. ? +−

📖 30 [*]

Vachier Lagrave, M. – Adams, M.

□ 33. ? ±

📖 31

Cramling, P. – Nemcova, K.

□ 14. ? ±/+−

📖 32 [*]

Ju, W. – Zhu, C.

□ 13. ? ±/+−

SOLUTIONS – CHAPTER 7

📖 1

21... ♘dc5! [21... ♘ec5 leads to the same] **22. dxc5 ♘xc5 23. ♖xc5 bxc5 24. ♘a3 c4∓/−+** Black will push ...f6, ...e5 with a nearly winning position.

In the game, Black played the slightly less convincing 24... f6∓ and later did not convert his advantage: ½-½ [72] Edouard, R [2620] – Ekstroem, R [2488] Novi Sad 2009.

📖 2

45. b5! axb5 46. ♕b6 The a-pawn will be promoted and Black does not have counter play against the white King. **46... ♕f8 47. a6 ♕b4 48. a7 ♕e1+ 49. ♔g2 ♕d2+ 50. ♔g1** 1-0 Kramnik, V [2801] – Vitiugov, N [2712] Paris 2013.

Black resigned in view of: 50. ♔g1 ♕e1+ 51. ♘f1+−

📖 3

20. ♖he1! White needs to bring a rook to f3! **20... ♖af8 21. ♖e3 ♗e8 22. ♖f3 ♖h2** [22... ♔d7 23. ♗e3±] **23. ♔e3+−**

1-0 [51] Van Kampen, R [2607] – Adams, M [2753] Hoogeveen 2013.

📖 4

17... d4! [17... a6?! 18. ♘d6 ♗xd6 19. cxd6±/±] **18. ♘xd4** [18. ♗xd4 ♘xd4 19. ♘xd4 ♕e7⯑] **18... ♗xd4 19. ♗xd4 ♗c2!! 20. ♕xc2** [20. ♗f6 ♕xf6 21. ♕xc2 ♘d4⯑] **20... ♘xd4 21. ♕a4 ♘xe2+ 22. ♘xe2 ♕g5 23. ♘d4 ♕xc5=** ½-½ [34] Kovalyov, A [2636] – Van Kampen, R [2636] Canada 2014.

📖 5

18. b4! axb4 [18... cxb4?! 19. ♗xb6+−] **19. a5 bxa5** [19... ♔b7 20. axb6 ♔xb6 21. ♘b3+−] **20. ♗xc5 ♘h6 21. ♖xa5±** 1-0 [26] Mamedyarov, S [2735] – Ragger, M [2688] Vienna 2015.

📖 6

29... ♗c6!

Not committing the pawn structure in any way!

Instead, Black continued with the much less convincing 29... c3?!∓ although he later won: 0-1 [37] Smirin, I [2655] – Radjabov, T [2738] Baku 2015.

30. bxc4 [30. ♖b1 ♖b7 31. b4 ♗a4 32. ♖cc1 c3−+] **30... ♗a4−+**

12. ♗a3‼ ♖xd1 13. ♖fxd1 ♕h5 [13...
♕c7 14. ♘b5 ♕d8 15. ♖xd8+ ♗xd8
16. ♖d1 ♘bd7 17. ♘cd6+−] **14. ♗xe7
♘bd7 15. ♗f3±** Black is paralyzed -
for example: **15... ♕f5 16. ♖ac1 ♘e8?
17. ♘e4! e5 18. ♘cd6 ♘xd6 19. ♘xd6
♕e6 20. ♘xc8+−** 1-0 Vachier Lagrave, M [2758] – Studer, N [2397]
Macedonia 2015.

40. a4!

A passed pawn is the key! Of course,
Black cannot just take "en passant"
due to the ♗c3-pin.

40... ♖e2 41. g4 ♖f2 42. ♖d3+− 1-0
[59] Harikrishna, P [2737] – Grandelius, N [2628] Germany 2015.

32. ♘f5!

32. ♖e1? ♘g7⇆ ½-½ [51] Maze, S [2614]
– Hamdouchi, H [2585] Drancy France
2016.

32... ♗xf5 [32... ♗xf2 33. ♘e7++−] **33.
♗xf5 gxf5 34. ♖xc5 ♖xc5 35. ♕e3+−**

31... ♖a2! 32. ♖xa2 [32. ♖c1 ♗xc4
33. ♖xc4 ♖h2 34. ♔g3 ♖d2 35. ♘f2
♗e3+−+] **32... ♗xc4 33. g5** [33. ♖ab2
♗h4! 34. ♔g2 ♖e1−+] **33... ♗xb3 34.
gxf6+ ♔xf6 35. ♖d2 ♗xd1+ 36. ♖xd1
♖e3+ 37. ♔f2 ♖e4−+** 0-1 [50] Krasenkow, M [2610] – Hammer, J [2695]
Sweden 2016.

40. ♖f4!

Instead, the game went: 40. ♕xc5?
bxc5= ½-½ [44] Khademalsharieh, S
[2403] – Harika, D [2511] Iran 2016.

40... ♖xe5 [40... ♕xe5 41. d7+−;
40... ♕xd4 41. ♖xd4 ♖xe5 42. d7+−]
41. d7+−

34. d5! e5 [34... exd5?! 35. ♗xg7+
♔xg7 36. ♕h7+ ♔f8 37. ♕h8#; 34...
cxd5?! 35. ♗xg7+ ♔xg7 36. ♕h7+ ♔f8
37. ♖xb5+−] **35. ♖c1+−** 1-0 [46] Kramnik, V [2801] – Giri, A [2798] Switzerland 2016.

30. e6‼

Instead, the game went: 30. ♘xe7+
♖xe7 31. ♖d8+ ♖xd8 32. ♖xd8+ ♖e8=

½-½ [42] Feller, S [2610] – Miron, L [2496] Cappelle la Grande 2016.

After the solution move 30. e6, Black's position collapses. Some examples...

30... ♛xe6

A) 30... ♞xe6 31. ♞e5 ♛b6 32. ♞xf7!? One of the many winning moves. *[32. ♖d7+–]* 32... ♚xf7 33. ♞xh6++–

B) 30... fxe6 31. ♞xh6+! Again one of many winning moves. *[31. ♞e5+–]* 31... gxh6 32. ♛g6+ ♚h8 33. ♞e5+–

C) 30... f6 31. ♞xh6+!+–

31. ♖d7

31. ♖e5 ♛c6 is not as convincing.

31... ♖b7 32. ♗xh6!

Also strong is: 32. ♖xe7!? ♖xe7 33. ♗xh6!? *[33. ♛xc5 is also winning]* 33... gxh6 34. ♖d6+–.

32... gxh6 33. ♖xe7 ♖xe7 34. ♖d6 ♛e4 35. ♞xe7+ ♛xe7 36. ♖xh6+–

📖 14

28... a5! 29. ♖xf7 [29. ♖ff3 axb4 30. cxb4 ♗d4∓] **29... ♖xf7 30. ♗b3** [30. ♛d5 ♖bf6 31. bxc5 h6–+] **30... ♖bf6–+** 0-1 [36] Trent, L [2455] – Efimenko, Z [2663] Germany 2016.

📖 15

27... ♗d3! 28. ♛b2 [28. cxd3 d4–+] **28... d4∓** 0-1 [39] Hector, J [2493] – Bacrot, E [2692] Germany 2016.

📖 16

20. ♞h4!!

20. ♗xb4 ♗xb4 21. ♞h4 g6 is much less clear: 22. ♛f3 *[22. ♞hxf5 gxf5 23. ♞xf5 ♛e6∞]* 22... ♗e7 23. ♞hxf5 gxf5 24. ♞xf5 ♚h8 25. ♛h5 ♛e6∓ 0-1 [32] Baskin, R [2329] – Neef, M [2406] Germany 2016.

20... g6 [20... ♗xh4 21. ♗xb4 ♗e7 22. ♗xe7 ♛xe7 23. ♞xf5+– Δ♛g4] **21. ♞hxf5! gxf5 22. ♞xf5 ♚h8 23. ♛h5!+–** followed by ♗h6, and Black is completely lost.

Also winning is: 23. ♗h6!? ♖g8 24. e6! ♛xe6 25. ♛xe6 fxe6 26. ♞xe7 ♖e8 27. ♖f7+–.

📖 17

26... c5!∓ [Δ... ♗c7, ...♖e4]

≤ 26... ♗e7 27. ♗f4 ♖c6 28. ♖d7 ♗d6= ½-½ [31] Demuth, A [2550] – Bluebaum, M [2628] Switzerland 2016.

After the excellent 26... c5, Black consolidates his queenside perfectly and will soon be able to take advantage of White's weak pawns. For example: 27.

g3 ♗c7 28. ♖d7 ♗d8 29. ♖b2 ♖e4 30. ♖bd2 ♗f6 31. ♖b7 ♖xc4 32. ♖a2 ♖a6∓.

📖 18

66. ♖h1! ♖xh1 [66... ♖gg2 67. ♖xh2 ♖xh2 68. ♘xc7+−] **67. ♗xg3 ♔f6 68. ♘xc7+−** 1-0 [95] Melkumyan, H [2646] − Veleski, R [2169] Gjakova 2016.

📖 19

14. ♘e5! ♗xd1 [14... ♘xe5 15. ♗xh7+! ♔xh7 16. ♕xh5+ ♔g8 17. dxe5±] **15. ♘xd7 ♖fd8 16. ♖axd1 ♖xd7 17. ♖fe1±** 1-0 [48] Salgado Lopez, I [2618] − Solodovnichenko, Y [2587] Drancy 2016.

📖 20

19. d5!

19. ♗f1 ♗xe4 20. ♗xc4 ♖xc4 21. ♕xc4 ♗d5 is much less clear.

19... ♗xd5

Black can try to resist with 19... ♗a4 but it will fail: 20. dxe6 fxe6 21. ♕b1 a5 22. ♗h3! axb4 *[22... ♖c6 23. ♘d6+ ♘xd6 24. ♖xe6+ ♔d8 25. ♖xd6 ♖xd6 26. ♗xd7+−]* 23. ♗xe6+−.

20. ♖ad1 ♔d8 21. ♘g5 ♗f6 22. ♗xd5 exd5 23. ♘e4

Even stronger was: 23. ♖xd5 ♕xd5 24. ♖d1 ♕xd1+ 25. ♕xd1+ ♔c7 26. ♘xf7+−.

23... ♗g7 24. ♖xd5 ♕xd5 25. ♖d1+− 1-0 [27] Caruana, F [2804] − Topalov, V [2761] Paris 2016.

📖 21

16... d4! 17. ♘xd4 [17. exd4 ♖ad8∓] **17... ♘xd4 18. exd4 ♖ad8∓** 0-1 [23] Lalith, B [2579] − Edouard, R [2648] Porticcio 2016.

📖 22

14. ♕h3!

Instead, the game went: 14. ♘xd5? ♗xh2+ 15. ♔xh2 ♕xd5 16. ♗xf6 ♕d6+∓ 1-0 [77] Bogner, S [2556] − Georgiadis, N [2470] Flims 2016.

14... h6 [14... ♗c8 15. ♕h4 h6 16. ♘xd5+−] **15. ♘xd5! ♗e5** [15... hxg5? 16. ♘xf6+ ♕xf6 17. ♕h7#] **16. ♘xf6+**

16. ♗xf6!? [Δ♕f5] 16... ♕xd5□ 17. ♗e4 ♕d6 18. ♗xe5 ♕xe5 19. ♕d7 is also better for White.

16... ♗xf6 17. ♗xh6! ♖e8 [17... dxe3? 18. ♗xg7!+−; 17... gxh6? 18. ♕xh6 ♖e8 19. ♗h7+ ♔h8 20. ♗g6+ ♔g8 21. ♕h7+ ♔f8 22. ♕xf7#] **18. ♗f4±**

📖 23

40. ♖b1!!

≤ 40. ♖6h5? ♔c6⇆ ½-½ [78] Dreev,A [2664] – Maghsoodloo,P [2501] Iran 2016.

40... e5 [40... ♗xh6 41. ♖b7+ ♔e8 42. ♖b8+ ♔d7 43. ♖xh8+−; 40... ♗e7 41. ♖b7+ ♔e8 42. ♖b8+ ♗d8 43. ♖g6 ♖fxh7 44. ♖xf6 ♔d7 45. ♖g6±; 40... ♗b4 41. c3±] **41. ♖b8 ♔e6 42. ♔b5 ♗g7 43. ♖g8+−** [Δc4] Black is completely dominated!

📖 24

37. a4! Just like the game Harikrishna – Grandelius (exercise 8 above). **37... ♕f4** [37... bxa3? 38. g5+−] **38. ♕d2+−** 1-0 [42] Rasmussen, A [2504] – Fressinet, L [2677] Denmark 2016.

White could also have played 38. a5+−.

📖 25

19... a4! 20. ♘xa4 [20. ♕c2? ♗b4−+] **20... ♕b4! 21. ♕xb4**

The game continued: 21. ♗c2 ♖xc2 22. ♕xc2 ♕xa4−+ 0-1 [58] Artemiev, V [2663] – Idani, P [2543] Baku 2016.

21... ♗xb4 22. ♘b2 ♖xa2∓

📖 26

13... ♘xc5! 14. dxc5 d4∓ 0-1 [46] Moncamp, G [2068] – Lagarde, M [2588] Marseille 2016.

📖 27

25... f5! 26. ♖xf5 [26. gxf5?! ♖xe4∓; 26. exf5? e4−+] **26... ♖xh3∓** 0-1 [53] Naiditsch, A [2687] – Henriquez Villagra, C [2517] Doha 2016.

📖 28

16... c3! 17. ♕h6 [17. ♘xc3?! ♕g5→ Δ... b4; 17. bxc3 b4⧡] **17... cxb2 18. ♖b1 b4 19. ♖xb2 ♖c8⧠** ½-½ [51] Vocaturo, D [2606] – Shvayger, Y [2413] Gibraltar 2017.

📖 29

27. ♘d2! h5 [27... ♗e7 28. ♘c4 ♗xc5? 29. ♘d6+ ♗xd6 30. exd6+−; 27... ♕a7 28. ♘c4 ♕xc5? 29. ♘d6++−] **28. ♘c4** [28. ♖b1!?+−] **28... h4** [28... ♕b8 avoiding ♖b1 was necessary, but for example White can play 29. ♕e1!? with a decisive advantage.] **29. ♖b1+−** Δ♘d6, ♖b7: 1-0 [37] Edouard, R [2613] – Vega Gutierrez, S [2406] Gibraltar 2017.

33. f5!

An excellent move, freeing the f4-square for the white Knight, and later possibly the white Bishop!

33... ♖xf5

The game continued: 33... ♗xf5 34. g4! hxg3 35. ♘xg3 ♗c2 36. ♖dd7! *[36. ♖d2? ♗g5=]* 36... ♖e5 37. ♘f4 ♗f6 38. ♘h5 ♖e1+ 39. ♔f2 ♗h4+ 40. ♘g3 ♖e6 41. ♗d6+?! *[41. ♖a7+−]* 41... ♖xd6 42. ♖xd6± 1-0 (55) Vachier Lagrave, M (2796) − Adams, M (2751) Gibraltar 2017.

34. ♘f4 ♖f6□ 35. ♘d5 ♗d8

The best defence. 35... ♖xf7 loses to 36. ♘xb6 ♗f5 37. ♘d7+ ♗xd7 38. ♖dxd7+− [Δ♖xe7].

36. ♘xf6 ♗xc7 37. ♖f1 gxf6 38. ♖xf6 ♗e6 39. ♗h6+ ♔e7 40. f8=♕+ ♖xf8 41. ♖xf8±

14. d5! exd5 15. ♗g5 ♘e4 [15... g6 16. ♖xe7! ♕xe7 17. ♘xd5+−] **16. ♘xe4 dxe4 17. ♕xe4 g6 18. ♕h4!**

Not as convincing is: 18. ♖ad1 ♕c8 19. ♕h4± 1-0 (52) Cramling, P (2434) − Nemcova, K (2359) Tehran 2017.

18... ♕d7 [18... ♗xg5 19. ♘xg5 h5 20. ♗b3+−; 18... h5 19. ♗b3+−] **19. ♖ad1 ♗xg5 20. ♘xg5 ♖xe1+ 21. ♖xe1 h5 22. ♗b3 ♖f8 23. ♘xf7** [23. ♘e4!?+−] **23... ♖xf7 24. ♕f6+−**

13. a4! (Δ♗a3)

13. ♕c2? ♘c6 14. ♕xe4?! ♘xd4 15. ♕xd4 0-0= ½-½ (51) Ju Wenjun (2583) − Zhu Chen (2419) Tehran 2017.

13... 0-0 [13... ♗d7 14. ♗a3±/+−] **14. ♘b5** White wins, e.g. **14... ♕b6** [14... ♕c6 15. ♗a3 ♖e8 16. ♖c1+−] **15. ♗e3 ♕a5 16. b4 ♕xb4 17. ♘c7+−**

Chapter 8

Find the missed move!

In this chapter, each position is accompanied by a series of moves which were played in a game. You must find the missed opportunity in this series of moves. The player whose move it is in the given position is the one who missed an opportunity.

In order to help you in your search, I will also give you the evaluation of the position if that missed move had been played.

The aim of this part of the book is to encourage you to concentrate on what is important, looking at the whole board, so you can spot key moments.

These exercises will also help you to find the right balance in your analysis: passing quickly over obvious things while making sure to notice possible surprises, so you develop a feeling for when the key moment has arrived.

The difficulty of these exercises ranges from medium to difficult, unless an asterisk indicates that the exercise is very difficult.

📖 1

Vallejo Pons, F. – Topalov, V.

30.♖f6 ♛d8 31.♛g5 ♘d2
32.♘h6+ ♔g7 33.♘f5+ ♔h8−+
[±]

📖 2

Negi, P. – Wen, Y.

33...♛d7 34.♖c8+ ♗d8
35.♘c5 ♛xe6 36.♖xd8++−
[−+]

📖 3 [*]

Nguyen, D. – Negi, P.

15.♛xe7 ♘xe5 16.♘xe5 ♗f6
17.♘d7 ♗xe7 18.♘xb6 axb6⩲
[±]

📖 4

Karpov, A. – Timman, J.

43.♖e8 ♛g6 44.♖d8 h4
45.♖d6 ♛f5 46.♛d1 ♖e6=
[+−]

5

Dominguez, L. – Kasimdzhanov, R.

24.♕b1 ♕b7
25.♕xe4 ♖c8 26.a4±
(+−)

6

Vachier Lagrave, M. – Aronian, L.

34...♖c2 35.♕d4 ♗h5
36.♗e4 ♖f2 37.♗xf5+−
(−+)

7

Koneru, H. – Gunina, V.

56...♕c7 57.♖e1 ♕c2
58.♕e2 ♕xe2 59.♖xe2 ♘e5±
(−+)

8 (*)

Kosintseva, T. – Ushenina, A.

18.♘xe5 ♕xf2+ 19.♔h1 ♕b6
20.♘xc6+ ♕xc6 21.♖e1±
(+−)

📖 9

Naiditsch, A. – Carlsen, M.

33...♘f6 34.♕xh4+ ♘h7 35.♗e6
♖f6 36.♗f5 ♖h6 37.♕e1+−
[∞]

📖 10

Steingrimsson, H. – Sargissian, G.

47.♔h1 e4 48.♘g1 e3
49.♕xe3 ♕xe3 50.fxe3 ♔f7∓
[+−]

📖 11

Bogner, S. – Laznicka, V.

23...♘xd5 24.♗xd5 ♗xd5
25.♘c3 ♘f6 26.♕xa6 ♕c7=
[−+]

📖 12

Rowson, J. – Jones, G.

35.♔h2 h4 36.gxh4 ♕xe4
37.♖g1 ♕f4+ 38.♔h1 ♕g3−+
[=]

Miton, K. – Ladva, O.

34...♛xf2 35.♝xd4 exd4 36.♛xd4
♜e2 37.♚g1 ♜d7 38.♜f1±
[=]

14 [*]

Aronian, L. – Kramnik, V.

18.♜xd7 ♝c6 19.b5 ♝xd7
20.♝xf6 gxf6∞
[+−]

15

Ushenina, A. – Gunina, V.

42.♜xf7 ♛g1+ 43.♚g3 ♜f1
44.♛e2 ♜e1 45.♛f2 ♜e3+−+
[+−]

16

Lagno, K. – Ju Wenjun, -.

27.♜xe3 ♜xc2 28.h4 h6
29.♝xg7+ ♚xg7∓
[±]

📖 17 [*]

Caruana, F. – Aronian, L.

37...♕d6 38.♖a1 ♕c5
39.♖b1 ♕a7=
[∓/−+]

📖 18

Landa, K. – Nyback, T.

30...c4 31.bxc4 ♘xc4
32.♘e5 ♘xe5 33.♗xe5 f6=
[−+]

📖 19

Chandra, A. – So, W.

32.♖b3 ♖h1 33.♔g4 ♔f8
34.♖g3 ♔g8−+
[+−]

📖 20

Milliet, S. – Smirnov, A.

50...♖xb6 51.♗c4 ♖d6 52.♗xe6 ♖xe6
53.♖xe6+ ♔xe6 54.h4 gxh3+ 55.♔xh3=
[−+]

Boruchovsky, A. – Grandelius, N.

50...♖d3+ 51.♔g2 ♖xd6
52.♖c7 ♘a5 53.♖xc2 ♘c6=
(−+)

Schwaegli, B. – Loetscher, R.

23.♘f6+ gxf6 24.♖h4 ♖fa8
25.♕h7+ ♔f8 26.♗xf6 ♔e8−+
(+−)

📖 23 (*)

Fressinet, L. – Carlsen, M.

31...♘xf2 32.R1xd4 cxd4
33.♖xd4 ♖e8 34.a6+−
(=)

📖 24

Megaranto, S. – Gelfand, B.

39.♕f1 e3 40.♕g2 ♕xg2+
41.♔xg2 ♘xg4−+
(+−)

📖 25

Matamoros F., C. – Vega Gutierrez, S.

15...♖c8 16.♘g5 b5
17.♘xe4 ♖xc4 18.♘xf6+=
[–+]

📖 26

Jones, G. – Kazhgaleyev, M.

43...♗xd5 44.♖e5 ♘e4
45.♖a6 ♗c6 46.♖xa7 ♘f6∞
[–+]

📖 27

Kramnik, V. – Vachier Lagrave, M.

16.♗h4 ♗c4 17.♕c2 ♗xf1
18.♖xf1 ♖ad8∓
[±]

📖 28

Naiditsch, A. – Borisek, J.

24.h4 ♕f7 25.h5 h6
26.♔h1 ♘e5 27.♕h3 ♘d7=
[±]

📖 29

Short, N. – Firouzja, A.

23.♗f6 ♘d7 24.♗xe5 ♘dxe5
25.♔h1±
[+−]

📖 30

Zude, E. – Marin, M.

32...♖g7 33.e6 ♔g8
34.♖c5 ♖d8 35.g3+−
[=]

📖 31

Studer, N. – Rambaldi, F.

38.♖d6 ♖c3 39.♖f1 ♕c7
40.♔h2 ♘d5 41.♖f3∞
[+−]

📖 32 [*]

Nakamura, H. – Giri, A.

39...♖xh3+ 40.♔g1 ♕xf3 41.♗xf3 ♘d3
42.♖e3 ♖xg3+ 43.♔h2+−
[∞]

📖 33

Ziska, H. – Krishna, C.

45...♞d6 46.♞e2 ♝c5 47.♛b2 ♛xb2
48.♖xb2 ♞d3 49.♖d2±
[∓]

📖 34

Vandenbussche, T. – Collutiis, D.

42...♖a8 43.♖e7 d3 44.♖h7+ ♚g8
45.♖g7+ ♚f8 46.♖f7+ ♚g8=
[−+]

📖 35

Lagarde, M. – Kantans, T.

27...♖ad8 28.0-0 ♖d1
29.g3 ♝xb2 30.♖xe6+−
[=]

📖 36

Galliamova, A. – Gunina, V.

30.e4 ♞xe4 31.♝xe4 ♖xd1+ 32.♞xd1
♛xe4 33.♚f1 ♛h1+−+
[White remains worse but alive!]

☐ 37

Edouard, R. – Tarhon, B.

24.♖g3 ♔h8 25.f5 ♖g8
26.♕e2⩲
[+−]

☐ 38 [*]

Kovalenko, I. – Dautov, R.

24.♘f4 ♗g4 25.♗xg4 ♕xg4
26.♖xd5 ♘xf2∞
[+−]

☐ 39 [*]

Kramnik, V. – Hou Yifan

37...♗d4+ 38.♔h1 ♗xe4 39.♕d2 ♗e3
40.♕d8 ♗xg2+ 41.♔h2+−
[−+]

☐ 40

Leko, P. – Ghaem Maghami, E.

25.♘g4 ♗g5 26.♖f1 ♕g3
27.♕e8+ ♔h7 ½-½
[+−]

📖 41

Henriquez Villagra, C. – Fressinet, L.

57...♕f1+ 58.♔h4 ♕xf3 59.♕xd4+
♔g8 60.♔g5 ♔h7 61.♕f4∞
[–+]

📖 42

Howell, D. – Mamedyarov, S.

18...e4 19.♘fxd4 ♖d8 20.♕b6
♕f8 21.♖a3 ♘d7 22.♕a7±
[–+]

📖 43

Dominguez Perez, L. – Ivanchuk, V.

39...♖xh3+ 40.gxh3 ♕xf2+ 41.♕g2
♕xd4 42.♖xe6 ♕f4+ 43.♕g3 ♕d2+=
[–+]

📖 44

Lalith Babu M R – Jakovenko, D.

40...♘g4+ 41.♔f3 ♘e5+ 42.♔f4
♘f7 43.♖a6+ ♔g7 44.♖a7+−
[–+]

📖 45

Leko, P. – Wei, Y.

18.♗f3 ♗xd4 19.♖xd4 ♕xf2
20.♖f4 ♕c5∓
(+−)

📖 46 (*)

Wojtaszek, R. – Van Wely, L.

32...♗xb2 33.♘b5 ♘c4
34.♘xd6 ♖xd6 35.♖b4+−
(±)

📖 47

Carlstedt, J. – Maze, S.

26.♖e1 ♖f8 27.♗g5 ♘d4
28.♗h6 ♗e6 29.♗xf8 ♔xf8⩲
(+−)

📖 48

Mastrovasilis, A. – Docx, S.

18.♗xc5 bxc5 19.♗d5 ♖fd8
20.♗xb7 ♕xb7=
(±)

SOLUTIONS – CHAPTER 8

📖 1

30. ♖f6 ♕d8 31. ♕g5 ♘d2? 32. ♘h6+??

<u>32. ♘e7+!</u> ♕xe7 *(32... ♔h8 33. ♕xe5±)* 33. ♖xg6+ fxg6 34. ♕xe7±

32... ♔g7 33. ♘f5+ ♔h8–+ 0-1 [34] Vallejo Pons, F [2666] – Topalov, V [2804] Leon 2006.

📖 2

33... ♕d7 34. ♖c8+ ♗d8 35. ♘c5 ♕xe6??

<u>35... ♕xc8!</u> 36. ♕xc8 e2 37. ♕xd8+ ♖f8 38. ♕d5+ ♔h8–+

36. ♖xd8+ 1-0 Negi, P [2622] – Wen, Y [2545] Mashhad 2011.

📖 3

15. ♕xe7 ♘xe5 16. ♘xe5 ♗f6 17. ♘d7?

<u>17. ♕xf8+!</u> ♔xf8 18. ♖xc8+ ♔g7 *(18... ♖xc8? 19. ♘d7++–)* 19. ♖xa8±

17... ♗xe7 18. ♘xb6 axb6⩱ ½-½ [30] Nguyen, D [2503] – Negi, P [2651] Philippines 2013.

📖 4

43. ♖e8 ♕g6 44. ♖d8 h4?? 45. ♖d6??

<u>45. f3!</u> ♖xe3 *(45... ♖e6 46. f5+–)* 46. ♖h8++–

45... ♕f5 46. ♕d1 ♖e6= ½-½ [55] Karpov, A [2619] – Timman, J [2600] Groningen 2013.

📖 5

24. ♕b1 ♕b7 25. ♕xe4 ♖c8 26. a4?± ½-½ [30] Dominguez, L [2751] – Kasimdzhanov, R [2706] Baku 2014.

<u>26. ♘e7+!</u> ♖xe7 27. ♗xe7 ♕xe7 28. ♕xd4+–

📖 6

34... ♖c2 35. ♕d4?? ♗h5! 36. ♗e4 ♖f2??

<u>36... ♖gxg2+!</u> 37. ♗xg2 ♗f3–+

37. ♗xf5+– 1-0 [39] Vachier Lagrave, M [2758] – Aronian, L [2797] China 2014.

📖 7

56... ♕c7 57. ♖e1 ♕c2 58. ♕e2 ♕xe2?

58... ♘f2+! 59. ♔g2 ♘d3!–+

59. ♖xe2 ♘e5± 1-0 [92] Koneru, H [2581] – Gunina, V [2522] China 2014.

📖 8

18. ♘xe5 ♕xf2+ 19. ♔h1 ♕b6 20. ♘xc6+?

20. ♕d4!! ♘f2+ 21. ♔g1 ♘h3+ 22. ♔f1+–

20... ♕xc6 21. ♖e1± 1-0 [44] Kosintseva, T [2483] – Ushenina, A [2494] China 2014.

📖 9

33... ♘f6 34. ♕xh4+ ♘h7 35. ♗e6 ♖f6?

35... c5!∞ Δ 35. ♗f5 ♖h6⇆

36. ♗f5 ♖h6 37. ♕e1+– 1-0 [68] Naiditsch, A [2706] – Carlsen, M [2865] Germany 2015.

📖 10

47. ♔h1 e4 48. ♘g1?

48. ♕d4!+–

48... e3 49. ♕xe3 ♕xe3 50. fxe3 ♔f7∓ 0-1 [76] Steingrimsson, H [2566] – Sargissian, G [2689] Reykjavik 2015.

📖 11

23... ♘xd5 24. ♗xd5 ♗xd5 25. ♘c3 ♘f6?

25... ♘xe5! 26. ♘xd5 ♘f3+! 27. ♕xf3 ♖xe1+ 28. ♖xe1 ♗xb2–+

26. ♕xa6 ♕c7= ½-½ [41] Bogner, S [2550] – Laznicka, V [2665] Reykjavik 2015.

📖 12

35. ♔h2 h4?? 36. gxh4??

36. ♖g7+! ♔xg7 37. ♕d7+ ♖8f7 38. ♕xg4+= White has a perpetual check.

36... ♕xe4 37. ♖g1 ♕f4+ 38. ♔h1 ♕g3–+ 0-1 [41] Rowson, J [2569] – Jones, G [2615] London 2015.

📖 13

34... ♕xf2 35. ♗xd4 exd4 36. ♕xd4 ♕e2 37. ♔g1 ♖d7?

37... ♖f2!=

38. ♖f1± 1-0 [91] Miton, K [2612] – Ladva, O [2404] Tallinn 2016.

📖 14

18. ♖xd7 ♗c6 19. b5?

<u>19. ♕c2!!</u> ♗xd7 *[19... ♘xd7 20. ♘g5+–]* 20. ♗xf6 gxf6 21. ♘g5+–

19... ♗xd7 20. ♗xf6 gxf6∞ 0-1 [43] Aronian, L [2792] – Kramnik, V [2801] Switzerland 2016.

📖 15

42. ♖xf7 ♕g1+ 43. ♔g3 ♖f1 44. ♕e2 ♖e1 45. ♕f2

<u>45. ♘d7!+–</u> [Δ♘f6+]

45... ♖e3+–+ 0-1 [52] Ushenina, A [2450] – Gunina, V [2496] China 2016.

📖 16

27. ♖xe3?

<u>27. ♗b4!</u> ♖xc4 28. ♖xe3±

27... ♖xc2 28. h4 h6 29. ♗xg7+ ♔xg7∓ ½-½ [45] Lagno, K [2529] – Ju Wenjun [2558] China 2016.

📖 17

37... ♕d6 38. ♖a1? ♕c5?

<u>38... ♖xd3!!</u> This move is winning. Of course, over the board, it was not easy to assess whether it was winning or not. However, Black definitely has the edge, which means it was a clear opportunity. 39. cxd3 ♕xd3+ 40. ♔e1 *[40. ♔g1 ♕c4!–+ The pawns will run!]* 40... ♕xe4+ 41. ♔f1 ♕d3+ 42. ♔e1 *[42. ♔g1?! ♕c4–+]* 42... ♕d2+ 43. ♔f1 c2 44. ♕b2+ ♔h7 45. ♖e1 *[45. ♔g1 b3 46. ♖f1 ♕f4 47. ♖e1 b4–+ Δ... ♕c4]* 45... ♕d1 46. f3 b3 47. ♔f2 b4! 48. ♕xb3 ♕xe1+–+

39. ♖b1 ♕a7= ½-½ [67] Caruana, F [2794] – Aronian, L [2786] Moscow 2016.

📖 18

30... c4 31. bxc4 ♘xc4?

<u>31... ♔f8!</u> 32. ♗d6 ♘xc4–+

32. ♘e5 ♘xe5 33. ♗xe5 f6= ½-½ [77] Landa, K [2626] – Nyback, T [2608] Germany 2016.

📖 19

32. ♖b3 ♖h1?? 33. ♔g4??

<u>33. ♖xe6+!</u> fxe6 34. ♕xe6+ ♔f8 35. ♖d3+–

33... ♔f8 34. ♖g3 ♔g8–+ 0-1 [40] Chandra, A [2477] – So, Wesley [2773] Saint Louis 2016.

50... ♖xb6 51. ♗c4 ♖d6

51... e3! 52. ♖xe6+ *[52. f4+ gxf3+ 53. ♔xf3 ♗d5+−+]* 52...♖xe6 53. ♗xe6 e2 54. f4+ gxf3+ 55. ♔f2 ♔xe6−+

52. ♗xe6 ♖xe6 53. ♖xe6+ ♔xe6 54. h4 gxh3+ 55. ♔xh3= 0-1 (61) Milliet, S (2353) – Smirnov, A (2479) Thailand 2016.

50... ♖d3+?

50... e4+! 51. ♔xe4 *[51. ♔g2 e3−+]* 51... ♖d4+ 52. ♔f3 ♘e5+−+

51. ♔g2 ♖xd6 52. ♖c7 ♘a5 53. ♖xc2 ♘c6 54. ♗a3 ½-½ Boruchovsky, A (2542) – Grandelius, N (2649) Gjakova 2016.

23. ♘f6+! gxf6 24. ♖h4! ♖fa8 25. ♕h7+??

25. ♕h8+ ♘xh8 26. ♗xf6+ ♘g6 27. ♖h8#

25... ♔f8 26. ♗xf6 ♔e8−+ 0-1 (33) Schwaegli, B (2276) – Loetscher, R (2429) Swirzerland 2016.

31... ♘xf2 32. ♖1xd4? cxd4 33. ♖xd4 ♖e8?

33... f5! 34. ♖c4 *[=34. ♗d5+ ♔g7 35. ♖c4 ♘xe4; 34. a6? ♘xe4∓; 34. e5?? ♘e4−+ Δ...♘d2+; 34. gxf6?? ♖xf6−+ Δ...♘xe4]* 34... ♘xe4 35. ♗d5+ ♔g7 36. ♖c7+ ♔h8 37. ♗xe4 fxe4 38. ♖xc3 ♖a8 39. ♖a3 e3=

34. a6+− 0-1 (58) Fressinet, L (2687) – Carlsen, M (2855) Paris 2016.

39. ♕f1 e3 40. ♕g2?

40. ♖xg5+! ♔xg5 41. ♕f5+ ♔h6 42. ♕h5+ ♔g7 43. ♘f5+ ♔f6 *[43... ♔g8 44. ♕g5+ ♘g6 45. ♘e7++−]* 44. ♕xh8+ ♔e6 45. ♕e8+ ♔f6 46. ♕d8+ ♔g6 47. ♘e7++−

40... ♕xg2+ 41. ♔xg2 ♘xg4−+ 0-1 (49) Megaranto, S (2535) – Gelfand, B (2734) Kazakhstan 2016.

15... ♖c8 16. ♘g5? b5 17. ♘xe4 ♖xc4?

17... ♗xe4! 18. ♗xe4 ♖xc4−+

18. ♘xf6+= ½-½ Matamoros Franco, C (2507) – Vega Gutierrez, S (2385) Italy 2016.

📖 26

43... ♗xd5 44. ♖e5 ♘e4 45. ♖a6?? ♗c6??

45... ♘c5!–+

46. ♖xa7 ♘f6∞ 1-0 [73] Jones, G [2650] – Kazhgaleyev, M [2582] Kazakhstan 2016.

📖 27

16. ♗h4 ♗c4 17. ♕c2?

17. ♗xe7! ♕c7 18. ♗d6! ♗xe2 19. ♗xc7 ♗xf1 20. ♔xf1±

17... ♗xf1 18. ♖xf1 ♖ad8∓ 0-1 [66] Kramnik, V [2812] – Vachier Lagrave, M [2789] Belgium 2016.

📖 28

24. h4 ♕f7? 25. h5?

25. ♕xe6! ♖xe6 *[25... ♕xe6 26. ♘xe6+–]* 26. ♘xe6±

25... h6 26. ♔h1 ♘e5 27. ♕h3 ♘d7= 1-0 [68] Naiditsch, A [2657] – Borisek, J [2576] Bled 2016.

📖 29

23. ♗f6 ♘d7? 24. ♗xe5?

24. ♘xe4! fxe4? 25. ♕g4++–

24... ♘dxe5 25. ♔h1± 1-0 [78] Short, N [2652] – Firouzja, A [2481] Iran 2016.

📖 30

32... ♖g7 33. e6 ♔g8 34. ♖c5?? ♖d8??

34... ♕d7!∓

35. g3+– 1-0 [52] Zude, E [2403] – Marin, M [2576] Denmark 2016.

📖 31

38. ♖d6 ♖c3 39. ♖f1 ♕c7? 40. ♔h2?

40. ♗xg6! fxg6 41. ♖d7 ♕c6 *[41... ♕xe5 42. ♖d8+ ♖xd8 43. ♕xd8+ ♔h7 44. ♖f7++–]* 42. ♖d8+ ♔g7 43. ♖f7+!! *[43. ♕f2!?+–]* 43... ♔xf7 44. ♕f2+ and mate to follow!

40... ♘d5 41. ♖f3∞ ½-½ [48] Studer, N [2462] – Rambaldi, F [2544] Switzerland 2016.

📖 32

39... ♖xh3+ 40. ♔g1 ♕xf3 41. ♗xf3 ♘d3?

41... ♘g4!∞

42. ♖e3 ♖xg3+ 43. ♔h2+– 1-0 [60] Nakamura, H [2791] – Giri, A [2769] Saint Louis USA 2016.

📖 33

**45... ♘d6 46. ♘e2 ♗c5 47. ♕b2??
♕xb2??**

47... ♘xc4!∓ Δ 48. bxc4? ♕e3−+

48. ♖xb2 ♘d3 49. ♖d2± 0-1 [89] Ziska, H [2546] – Krishna, C [2401] Abu Dhabi 2016.

📖 34

42... ♖a8??

42... ♖g7!−+

**43. ♖e7 d3 44. ♖h7+ ♔g8 45. ♖g7+
♔f8 46. ♖f7+ ♔g8= ½-½ [48]** Vandenbussche,T [2401] – Collutiis,D [2441] Baku 2016.

📖 35

27... ♖ad8??

27... ♘d4!= Δ 28. ♖xe5?? ♘c2+ 29. ♔f1
♖d1#

**28. 0-0 ♖d1 29. g3 ♗xb2 30.
♖xe6+−1-0 [46]** Lagarde,M [2593] – Kantans,T [2476] Bastia 2016.

📖 36

**30. e4 ♘xe4 31. ♗xe4 ♖xd1+? 32.
♘xd1?**

---

32. ♔g2! would have been a nasty surprise, as Black is better but suddenly does not have a forced win: 32... ♕d7!? *(32... ♕a7 33. ♕xa7 ♗xe4+ 34. ♔h3 ♗xa7 35. ♘xd1∓)* 33. ♕xa8 ♖d2 34. ♘d1! ♗d4 *(34... ♖xd1 35. ♗xe5+ f6 36. ♗c3∓)* 35. ♗c6! ♕d6 36. ♗xd4 ♕xd4 37. ♗a4 ♕xb4 38. ♗e8! ♖xd1 39. ♕f3 ♕d6 40. ♕xf7+ ♔h8 41. h4 and White should hold.

32... ♕xe4−+ 0-1 [33] Galliamova, A [2450] – Gunina, V [2535] Novosibirsk 2016.

📖 37

24. ♖g3 ♔h8 25. f5?

25. ♖xg7! ♔xg7 26. ♗f6+ ♔g8 *(26...
♔f8 27. ♕h7+−)* 27. ♖f3+−

25... ♖g8 26. ♕e2⩱ 1-0 [37] Edouard, R [2628] – Tarhon, B [2300] Reading 2016.

📖 38

24. ♘f4 ♗g4?! 25. ♗xg4?

25. ♖xd5! ♖xd5 26. ♘xd5 ♗xf3 *(26...
♕xd5 27. ♗xe4+−)* 27. ♘e7+ ♔h8 28.
♘g6+! hxg6 29. ♕xf8+ ♔h7 30. ♕xg7#

25... ♕xg4 26. ♖xd5 ♘xf2∞ ½-½ [36] Kovalenko, I [2664] – Dautov, R [2607] Germany 2016.

📖 39

37... ♗d4+ 38. ♔h1 ♗xe4 39. ♕d2 ♗e3??

39... ♕d7! 40. ♔h2 ♕g7 41. ♔h1 ♕g3–+

40. ♕d8 ♗xg2+ 41. ♔h2+–

📖 40

25. ♘g4 ♗g5 26. ♖f1 ♕g3?? 27. ♕e8+??

27. ♘f6+! ♗xf6 28. ♗xe6+ ♔f8 29. ♖xf6+ ♔e7 30. ♖f7+ ♔xe6 31. ♘c5+ ♔d6 32. ♕h6+ ♘g6 33. ♖f6++–

27... ♔h7 28. ♕h5+ ♔g8 29. ♕e8+? ♔h7 ½-½ Leko, P (2693) – Ghaem Maghami, E (2574) Doha 2016.

📖 41

57... ♕f1+ 58. ♔h4 ♕xf3 59. ♕xd4+?? ♔g8??

59... f6! 60. ♕d7+ ♔h6–+

60. ♔g5 ♔h7 61. ♕f4∞ 1-0 (107) Henriquez Villagra,C (2517) – Fressinet,L (2672) Doha 2016.

📖 42

18... e4 19. ♘fxd4 ♖d8?

19... exd3 20. exd3 ♘d7–+ Attacking the d4-knight and defending the b8-

rook! Of course, 19... ♘d7 also works, although exchanging on d3 first is even stronger.

20. ♕b6 ♕f8 21. ♖a3 ♘d7 22. ♕a7±

½-½ (86) Howell, D (2644) – Mamedyarov, S (2768) Doha 2016.

📖 43

39... ♖xh3+! 40. gxh3 ♕xf2+?

40... ♖xh3+! 41. ♔xh3 ♕h1+ 42. ♔g3 ♕g1+–+

41. ♕g2 ♕xd4 42. ♖xe6 ♕f4+ 43. ♔g3 ♕d2+= ½-½ (46) Dominguez Perez, L (2739) – Ivanchuk, V (2747) Doha 2016.

📖 44

40... ♘g4+ 41. ♔f3 ♘e5+ 42. ♔f4?? ♘f7??

42... ♖g4+! 43. ♗xg4 g5#

43. ♖a6+ ♔g7 44. ♖a7+– 1-0 (45) Lalith, B (2587) – Jakovenko, D (2704) Doha 2016.

📖 45

18. ♗f3 ♗xd4? 19. ♖xd4??

19. ♕b3! ♕g5 20. ♕xb7+ ♔d7 21. ♗c6+ ♔e7 22. ♕xc7+ ♔f6 23. ♖xd4 ♕c5 24. ♖f4+ ♗f5 25. ♖d1+–

19... ♛xf2 20. ♖f4 ♛c5∓ 1-0 [24] Leko, P [2693] – Wei Yi [2707] Doha 2016.

📖 46

32... ♗xb2 33. ♘b5 ♘c4??

<u>33... ♖c6!</u> That could also have been an excellent example for the chapter "Play the right move under pressure!". 34. ♖xb6 *[34. ♗xb6 ♗e5=]* 34... ♖xb6 35. ♗xb6 ♖b7 36. ♖b1 a3 37. ♔f1 ♖xb6 38. ♘xa3 ♖a6 39. ♘c4±

34. ♘xd6 ♖xd6 35. ♖b4+− 1-0 [46] Wojtaszek, R [2750] – Van Wely, L [2695] Wijk aan Zee 2017.

📖 47

26. ♖e1 ♖f8 27. ♗g5?

<u>27. g4!</u> ♛xg4+ *[27... ♗xg4 28. ♖h2 ♛f5 29. ♛h6+−]* 28. ♔h2+−

27... ♘d4 28. ♗h6 ♗e6 29. ♗xf8 ♔xf8⩱ ½-½ [33] Carlstedt, J [2413] – Maze, S [2613] Gibraltar 2017.

📖 48

18. ♗xc5 bxc5 19. ♗d5 ♖fd8? 20. ♗xb7?

<u>20. ♗xf7+!</u> ♔xf7 21. ♘g5+ ♔e8□ *[21... ♔g8? 22. ♛c4++−; 21... ♔f6? 22. ♘xh7+ ♔f7 23. ♛c4+ e6 24. ♘g5++−]* 22. ♛c4 e5□ 23. ♘e6 *[≤ 23. ♛g8+ ♗f8 24. ♛xf8+ ♔xf8 25. ♘e6+ ♔e7 26. ♘xc7 ♖xd1+ 27. ♖xd1 ♖b8⇄]* 23... ♖xd1+ 24. ♖xd1 ♛c6□ After this move White does not have a forced win, but of course the position is one-sided and in White's favour. *[24... ♛e7? 25. ♛b5++−]* 25. ♘xg7+ ♔f8 26. ♘e6+ ♔e7 27. f3 ♛xe6 28. ♛xc5+ ♔e8 29. ♖d6 ♛f5 30. e4 *[30. ♛b5+ ♔e7□ and again, White is better but does not have a forced win.]* 30... ♛c8 31. ♛xe5+ ♔f7 32. ♛d4 ♖a6□ 33. ♖d7+ ♔e6□ 34. ♖xh7 ♖d6□ 35. ♛e3± White has four pawns for a piece, and a safer King!

20... ♛xb7= ½-½ [42] Mastrovasilis, A [2551] – Docx, S [2405] Gibraltar 2017.

Chapter 9

Evaluate the opportunity!

For each exercise in this chapter, I will suggest a possible move. You must say whether the move is good or bad and evaluate the resulting position in the same way as a chess engine: White is winning, Black is winning, White is better, Black is better, or the position is equal or un-clear.

You must find the key continuation and explain why the suggested move does or does not work.

This is intended to replicate a game situation, when you must analyse a critical candidate move. The difficulty of these exercises ranges from medium to difficult, unless an asterisk indicates that the exercise is very difficult.

1

Sjugirov, S. – Karjakin, S.

■ 42...♖xc3?

2

Lupulescu, C. – Bogner, S.

□ 12.♕xc6+?

3

Hoffmann, M. – Cornette, M.

■ 16...♗xd5?

4

Bacrot, E. – Baramidze, D.

□ 27.♘ce4?

5

Topalov, V. – Giri, A.

■ 33...♞xf2?

 6 [*]

Nakamura, H. – Vachier-Lagrave, M.

■ 32...gxf3?

 7

Shyam, S. – Maze, S.

□ 13.♞xe5?

 8

Ma, Z. – Ivanchuk, V.

■ 18...♞c5?

📖 9

Arvola, B. – Kryvoruchko, Y.

■ 29...♖c1+?

📖 10

Amin, B. – Gasanov, E.

□ 33.c5?

📖 11

Howell, D. – Jumabayev, R.

□ 17.♘f6+?

📖 12

Fier, A. – Brunner, N.

□ 39.♖xd5?

📖 13

Karavade, E. – Bailet, P.

■ 33...♖xb2+?

📖 14

Hector, J. – Demuth, A.

■ 13...b5?

📖 15 (*)

Brochet, P. – Vaisser, A.

□ 18.♖xe5?

📖 16

Sokolov, I. – Mousavi, S.

□ 17.♗xh6?

📖 17 [*]

Edouard, R. – Tabatabaei, M.

□ 20.e5?

📖 18

Vachier-Lagrave, M. – Anand, V.

□ 30.♘xe6?

📖 19

Maze, S. – Mastrovasilis, D.

■ 33...♗xf2+?

📖 20

L'Ami, E. – Adhiban, B.

■ 36...♗xc4?

📖 21

Pultinevicius, P. – Moroni, L.

■ 42...♛xd4?

📖 22

Kenneskog, T. – Vanheirzeele, D.

■ 24...♞xf3+?

📖 23

Carlsen, M. – Karjakin, S.

■ 21...♞xf2+?

📖 24 [*]

Reinhart, E. – Riff, J.

□ 22.♞xe5?

SOLUTIONS – CHAPTER 9

📖 1

42... 🏰xc3!

Good! Black is (much) better.

43. ♛e6+

The best defence would have been: 43. f6 ♛xg3+ 44. ♛xg3 🏰gxg3 45. ♗e6+ [45. f7 🏰cf3+ 46. ♚e2 🏰xf4 47. 🏰xh5 ♚d7−+] 45... ♚d8 46. 🏰xh5 🏰cf3+ 47. ♚e2 🏰e3+ 48. ♚f2 🏰xe6 49. ♚xg3 🏰xf6 and Black should be winning.

43... ♚b7 44. ♛xg8 🏰c2+! The point! **45. ♗xc2** [45. ♚f3? ♛c3+ 46. ♚e4 🏰e2+ 47. ♚d5 ♛c5#; 45. ♚f1? ♛a1#] **45... ♛xg8−+** 0-1 (66) Sjugirov, S [2653] – Karjakin, S [2772] Loo 2014.

📖 2

12. ♛xc6+??

Bad! Black wins.

12. gxf3 was better.

12... ♞d7 13. gxf3 🏰c8 14. ♛a4 🏰xc1!−+ 0-1 (24) Lupulescu, C [2660] – Bogner, S [2587] Dubai 2014.

White loses because of: 14... 🏰xc1 15. 🏰xc1 ♛g5+−+.

📖 3

16... ♗xd5!

Good! Black is better.

Instead, the game went 16... ♛h4? 17. ♞xe4 fxe4 18. f4∞ ½-½ [42] Hoffmann, M [2447] – Cornette, M [2548] Belgium 2014.

17. ♗c4? The only answer not to be simply a pawn down, but... **17... 🏰xg2+! 18. ♚xg2** [18. ♚h1 🏰g1+! 19. ♚xg1 ♛g5+ 20. ♚h1 ♞xf2#] **18... ♛g5+ 19. ♚h1 ♞xf2#**

📖 4

27. ♞ce4?

Bad! The position becomes a draw.

⌓ 27. fxg4±

27... gxf3 28. 🏰h8+ ♚g7 29. 🏰h7+

Now the key of this exercise: did you notice that 29. 🏰dh1?? fails because of 29... ♞d2+! 30. ♞xd2 ♗f5+−+?

29... ♚f8 30. 🏰h8+ ♚g7 31. 🏰h7+ ½-½ Bacrot, E [2711] – Baramidze, D [2594] Germany 2015.

33... ♘xf2!

Good! Black wins.

34. ♗xe2 ♘xh3+ 35. ♔f1 ♕d5! The point! **36. ♗h5** [36. ♔e1 ♕h1+ 37. ♗f1 ♕f3 38. ♖b2 ♕xg3+ 39. ♔f2 ♖e8+ 40. ♗e2 ♘f4–+] **36... ♕h1+ 37. ♔e2 ♕g2+ 38. ♔e1 ♖e8+ 39. ♔d1 ♘f2+ 40. ♔c2 ♘e4+** 0-1 Topalov, V [2803] – Giri, A [2778] Loncon 2015.

White resigned in view of: 40... ♘e4+ 41. ♔d3 ♕d2+ 42. ♔c4 ♖c8+ 43. ♕c5 ♖xc5#.

32... gxf3!

Good! Black is winning.

Instead, the game went 32... ♗xc4? 33. ♘xc4 ♘d5∞ ½-½ [57] Nakamura, H [2793] – Vachier Lagrave, M [2765] London 2015.

33. ♗h6 ♘e4+ 34. ♔e3 [34. ♔f1 ♔h7! 35. ♗xg7 ♗e6!?–+] **34... ♔h7! 35. ♗xg7 f2!** [35... f6!? is also good] **36. ♖g2 ♘d4–+**

13. ♘xe5?

Bad! Black is winning.

13... ♖xe5! 14. ♘c4

After 14. dxe5 ♕h4 Black gets a winning attack: 15. ♖e3□ [15. ♖f1 ♗xh3–+] 15... ♗xe3 16. fxe3 ♗xh3 17. ♘f3 [17. gxh3 ♕g3+ 18. ♔f1 ♕xh3+ 19. ♔e1 ♕h4+ 20. ♔f1 ♘xe5–+] 17... ♕g3 18. ♕f1 ♘xe5–+

14... ♖g5 15. ♗xg5 ♕xg5–+ 0-1 [38] Shyam, S [2485] – Maze, S [2582] Spain 2015.

18... ♘c5?

Bad! White is better.

⌓ 18... ♗e7=

19. ♗xf8! ♘xb3 20. ♖cd1 ♕xf8 21. ♕c4!± ½-½ [37] Ma Zhonghan – [2463] – Ivanchuk, V [2710] Doha 2015.

White wins material as the ♗ on h4 and the ♘ on b3 can't both be defended.

29... ♖c1+!

Good! Black wins.

30. ♘f1 [30. ♖d1 ♕xe3!–+ The important trick to see!] **30... ♕f5 31. g4** [31. ♕d8+ ♔h7 32. ♕d3 ♕xd3 33. ♖xd3 ♗e2–+] **31... ♖xf1+** 0-1 Arvola, B [2328] – Kryvoruchko, Y [2711] Al Ain 2015.

White resigned in view of: 31... ♖xf1+ 32. ♔xf1 ♕b1+–+.

📖 10

33. c5!

Good! White is winning.

33. h4? ♗g1+ 34. ♔h3 ♕d7+∞ ½-½ [68] Amin, B [2665] – Gasanov, E [2485] Al Ain 2015.

33... ♕xd6□ 34. ♕c3! [=34. ♕b4] **34... ♗xc5** [34... ♕e7? 35. ♕xe1+–] **35. ♕xe1+–**

📖 11

17. ♘f6+!

Good! White wins.

17. ♗e7 brings an advantage, but the suggested move just wins.

17... gxf6 18. ♗xf6 ♘g6 19. ♕h5 [19. ♕d2 leads to the same.] **19... e5 20. ♖c6!+–** 1-0 [27] Howell, D [2685] – Jumabayev, R [2607] Tallinn 2016.

20. ♗c6 also wins.

📖 12

39. ♖xd5

Good! White is winning.

39... g4 40. g3! The important move to see! **40... ♘xg3 41. ♖d8+ ♔h7 42. ♕a8 ♘e2+ 43. ♔g2 ♘f4+** [43... ♕h3+ 44. ♔f2 ♕h2+ 45. ♔e1+–] **44. exf4 ♕h3+ 45. ♔f2 ♕h2+ 46. ♔e3 ♕g3+ 47. ♔e4+–**

The white King escapes and White has many ways to win, but the end of the game was quite nice...

47... ♕e1+ 48. ♔d5 ♕d1+ 49. ♔c6 ♕f3+ 50. ♔d6 ♕xa8 51. ♖xa8 g3 52. ♔xe7 g2 53. ♔f7! g1=♕ 54. e7 ♕xa1 55. ♖h8+! 1-0 [55] Fier Takeda, A [2608] – Brunner, N [2438] France 2016.

Black resigned in view of: 55. ♖h8+ ♔xh8 56. e8=♕ + ♔h7 57. ♕g8+ ♔h6 58. ♕h8#.

📖 13

32... ♖xb2+!

Good! Black wins.

33. ♖xb2 ♖xb2+ 34. ♔xb2 ♕d2+ 35. ♔b1 a3 36. ♕e2 ♕b4+ 37. ♔a1 [37. ♔c2 ♕b2+ 38. ♔d1 ♕c1#] **37... ♕c3+ 38. ♔b1 ♗d2!** 0-1 Karavade, E [2400] – Bailet, P [2509] France 2016.

13... b5?

Bad! White is better.

The right choice was the simple 13... ♗xc5 14. ♘xf5 exf5 15. ♗d5 0-0 16. 0-0 b5∞ ½-½ (49) Hector, J [2493] – Demuth, A [2550] Denmark 2016.

14. ♘xb5 axb5 15. ♕xb5 ♖a5 16. ♖d8+! The point! Otherwise Black would be better. **16... ♕xd8 17. ♕xc6+ ♕d7 18. ♕xd7+ ♔xd7 19. ♗b6±**

18. ♖xe5?

Bad! Black is winning.

A much better choice was: 18. ♗xh6 ♗f4 *[18... gxh6? 19. ♕xh6 ♖fe8 20. ♕g5+±]* 19. ♗xf4 ♕xf4 20. ♔g1=

18... ♕xe5!

In the game Black failed to find the 'winning defence' and played 18... hxg5?? 19. ♖xg5+− 1-0 (35) Brochet, P [2379] – Vaisser, A [2509] Drancy 2016.

19. f4 ♘e4!! What a move! **20. ♕e3** [20. fxe5 ♘f2+−+] **20... ♕d6 21. ♕xe4 f5!−+**

17. ♗xh6!

Good! White is winning.

Instead, the game went: 17. ♘xd5? ♕xd5 18. ♖e3→ ½-½ (27) Sokolov, I [2642] – Mousavi, S [2432] Iran 2016.

17... gxh6 18. ♕xh6 ♕xb2 19. ♘xd5 exd5 20. ♖ad1!! The point! **20... ♕c2** [20... ♗f5 21. ♖e3 ♕c2 22. ♖g3+ ♗g6 23. ♖e1+−] **21. ♖d3+−**

20. e5?

Bad! The position becomes unclear.

After 20. exd5! Black is far away from getting enough compensation: 20... ♖fe8 *[20... ♖xb2 21. ♗d2 ♖e8+ 22. ♗e2+−]* 21. ♔f2 ♖xb2+ 22. ♖xb2 ♕xc3 23. ♖e2 *[23. ♕c1!? ♖xe3 24. ♖b8+ ♔h7 25. ♕xc3 ♖xc3 26. ♗b3 c4 27. ♖c8!+−]* 23... ♕xc4 24. ♕b3+−.

20... dxc4 21. exf6 ♖xb2! 22. ♗d2

After 22. ♖xb2 ♕xc3+ 23. ♕d2 ♕xf6 24. ♖c2 ♕xf3 25. ♖f1 ♕e4≅ the position is very tricky and probably around equal! Black has many pawns and White has a problem to run away with his King.

22... ♖e8+ 23. ♘e4 ♕xd2+! 24. ♕xd2 ♖xb1+ 25. ♕d1 ♖xd1+ 26. ♔xd1 ♗h8!

27. g4 g5∓ Δ...♖e6: ½-½ (41) Edouard, R (2639) – Tabatabaei, M (2481) Biel 2016.

📖 18

30. ♘xe6??

Bad! Black is winning.

30. ♗xd5 was a better option: 30... exd5 31. ♕h3±

30... ♗xe6 31. ♗xd5 e3! 32. ♗xe3 ♗xd5–+ 0-1 (46) Vachier Lagrave, M (2819) – Anand, V (2770) USA 2016.

📖 19

33... ♗xf2+!

Good! Black gets a draw.

34. ♔h2 ♗g1+! The important move to see! **35. ♔xg1□ ♕d4+ 36. ♔f2□ ♕a1+=** ½-½ (43) Maze, S (2617) – Mastrovasilis, D (2601) Baku 2016.

📖 20

36... ♗xc4!

Good! Black is much better.

37. ♗f3

White cannot go for 37. ♗xf7+? because of: ♖xf7 38. ♖xd6 ♖f1#.

37... ♖xd1+ 38. ♗xd1 ♗b5∓ 0-1 (66) L'Ami, E (2611) – Adhiban, B (2671) Baku 2016.

📖 21

42... ♕xd4!

Good! Black is winning.

Instead, the game went: 42... ♗g4 43. e5⇆ 1-0 (68) Pultinevicius, P – Moroni, L Khanty-Mansiysk 2016.

43. ♕xd4 ♖xd2 44. ♕c5 ♗g4!–+

The important move to see. The Bishop will go to h3 and White eventually gets mated.

📖 22

24... ♘xf3+!

Good! Black is winning.

24... ♗g6? 25. ♕xd5 ♘c4!⩲ 0-1 (34) Kenneskog, T (2332) – Van Heirzeele, D (2120) Novi Sad 2016.

25. ♗xf3 ♗xf3 26. ♘xf3 ♕xe3+ 27. ♔g2 ♖c2+ 28. ♔h3 ♕h6+ 29. ♔g4 ♕e6+ 30. ♔h4 ♕f6+ 31. ♔h3 ♕f5+ 32. ♔h4 g5+! 33. ♔h5 (33. ♘xg5 ♖xh2+ 34. ♘h3 ♖xh3#) **33... ♕xf3+ 34. ♔xg5 f6+ 35. ♔h6 ♖xh2#**

21... ♞xf2+!

Good! This leads to a draw.

21... ♞g5?! 22. h4± 1-0 [75] Carlsen, M [2853] – Karjakin, S [2772] New York 2016.

22. ♔g2 ♛f7□ [Δ...♞f4+] 23. ♔g1

23. ♛e2 ♞h4+ 24. ♔g1 *(24. gxh4?? ♛g6+–+)* 24... ♞h3+ 25. ♔h1 ♞f2+=

23... ♛f6□ [Δ...♛g5] 24. ♔g2

A] 24. h4? ♞f4! 25. gxf4 ♛xf4–+

B] 24. ♛e2?! ♞h3+ 25. ♔g2 ♞hf4+ 26. gxf4 ♞xf4+ 27. ♖xf4 ♛xf4∓

C] 24. ♖ae1 ♛g5 25. ♛xg5 ♞h3+ 26. ♔g2 ♞xg5 27. ♖xf8+ ♞xf8 28. ♞g4 ♞d7 29. exd5 exd5 30. ♞xe5=

24... ♛f7=

22. ♞xe5!

Good! White is winning.

22. ♖xc6?! ♔g7 23. ♗b2 ♖ac8 24. ♖xc8?! ♖xc8∓ 0-1 [46] Reinhart, E – Riff, J Baden Baden 2017.

22... ♗g5□

22... dxe5 23. ♛xh6+ ♔g8 24. ♖g3+ ♗g6 25. ♖xg6+ fxg6 26. ♛xg6+ ♔f8 27. ♖d3 e4 and here White has many ways to conclude the game, like 28. ♖g3+–.

23. ♛e2! dxe5

23... ♗xc1 24. ♞xc6 ♛d7 25. ♖dxc1+–

24. ♗xg5 hxg5 25. ♛xe5

White is winning, for example:

25... ♗e6

25... ♔g6 26. ♖xc6+ ♗e6 27. ♖xe6+ fxe6 28. ♛xe6+ ♔h5 29. ♖d6+–

26. ♛xg5+–

Chapter 10

Make the right choice!

In each exercise in this chapter, I will suggest two possible moves. One of them is a blunder! You must decide which is right and, most importantly, the reason why the other one is a mistake.

Generally, if the two moves suggested are quite similar, you must find the key continuation in both lines, in order to discover a final important nuance. If the two moves are very different, you must find a clear refutation of one of them.

This chapter is intended to help you to work on your calculation skills, while developing your sense of danger when you need to rule out a move which seemed good at first glance.

The difficulty of these exercises ranges from medium to difficult, the most challenging ones being marked with an asterisk.

1

Zhao, X. – Vachier Lagrave, M.

■ 24...♗xf3 / 24...♘xf3

 2

Ivanchuk, V. – Topalov, V.

□ 37.♕xb7 / 37.♕f7+

 3

Edouard, R. – Fressinet, L.

■ 17...b5 / 17... 0-0

 4

Vachier Lagrave, M. – Koch, J.

□ 54.c6 / 54.♘e5

5

Efimenko, Z. – Forster, R.

□ 27.♖f1 / 27.♘e4

 6 [*]

Kamsky, G. – Shankland, S.

■ 10...♗xd7 / 10...♕xd7

 7

Karpov, A. – Graf, F.

□ 51.♖dd1 / 51.♘xg7

 8 [*]

Edouard, R. – Claesen, P.

■ 17...g5 / 17...♕b6

📖 9

Mueller, M. – Braun, A.

☐ 30.h5 / 30.g4

📖 10

Jobava, B. – Alekseenko, K.

☐ 33.♖d1 / 33.♖e1

📖 11 (*)

Artemiev, V. – Petrosian, T.

■ 28...♕b5 / 28...♖xc5

📖 12

Shirov, A. – Simacek, P.

■ 32...♕a7 / 32...♕a2

📖 13 (*)

Sethuraman, S. – Sengupta, D.

■ 14...♖fc8 / 14...♖ac8

📖 14

Schiendorfer, E. – Fischer, M.

□ 33.♖xd3 / 33.♔e3

📖 15 (*)

Naiditsch, A. – Demuth, A.

□ 24.♗a3 / 24.♕xf5

📖 16

Edouard, R. – Darini, P.

□ 37.♔e1 / 37.♔e2

📖 17

Hammer, J. – Carlstedt, J.

□ 26.♔e1 / 26.♔e2

📖 18

Xu Xiangyu, -. – Zhao, C.

□ 51.♕e5+ / 51.♕d4+

📖 19

Mareco, S. – Nakamura, H.

□ 64.c7 / 64.♔g3

📖 20

Cori, J. – Salgado Lopez, I.

□ 39.♗b5 / 39.♘c4

21 (*)

Shankland, S. – Sethuraman, S.

■ 31...罝a3 / 31...豐f7

 22

Pultinevicius, P. – Moroni, L.

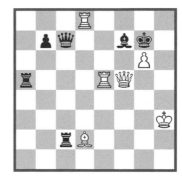

■ 60...罝xd2 / 60...罝xe5

📖 23

Charochkina, D. – Gunina, V.

■ 11...dxc4 / 11...🐴xc5

📖 24

Carlsen, M. – Bosiocic, M.

■ 14...f5 / 14...豐xd1+

SOLUTIONS – CHAPTER 10

📖 1

A) 24... ♗xf3! 25. ♗xf3 *(25. gxf3 f5–+)* 25... ♖xe1+ 26. ♔xe1 ♘xf3+–+ 0-1 [29] Zhao, X [2478] – Vachier Lagrave, M [2525] Shenzheng 2005.

B) 24... ♘xf3? 25. gxf3 ♗h3+ 26. ♔e2 f5 27. ♖hg1+ ♔f6 28. ♖g3⇆

📖 2

A) 37. ♕f7+! ♔d8 38. ♕xb7 *(38. ♖d1+!? ♔d5 39. ♕xe6 ♕e3+ 40. ♔b1 ♕e4+ 41. ♔a1!? ♕c7 42. ♕xd5 ♕xd5 43. ♖xd5 ♗f8=)* 38... ♕e3+ 39. ♔d1 ♕d3+ 40. ♔e1 ♕e3+=

B) 37. ♕xb7?? ♕e3+ 38. ♔c2 *(38. ♔d1 ♖d8+–+)* 38... ♕e2+ 39. ♔b3 ♕c4+ 40. ♔c2 b3+! 41. ♔d2 *(41. axb3 ♕e2+–+)* 41... ♖d8+ 42. ♔e1 ♖d1+! 43. ♔xd1 ♕xf1+ 44. ♔d2 ♕f4+ 45. ♔d1 bxa2–+ 0-1 [54] Ivanchuk, V [2746] – Topalov, V [2812] Bulgaria 2009.

📖 3

A) 17... 0-0 18. dxc6 bxc6 19. ♕c2±

B) 17... b5? 18. ♖xc6! ♖xc6 19. ♗xb5+– 1-0 [67] Edouard, R [2597] – Fressinet, L [2667] Nimes 2009.

📖 4

A) 54. ♘e5+–

B) 54. c6?? ♖xd3 55. c7 ♖d1+ 56. ♔g2 ♖d2+ 57. ♔h3 ♘e4! 58. c8=♕ ♘f2+ 59. ♔g2 ♘g4+! 60. ♔h1 *(60. ♔f1 ♘h2+ 61. ♔e1 ♘f3+=; 60. ♔f3 ♘h2+ 61. ♔e3 ♘f1+=; 60. ♔g1 ♖d1+=)* 60... ♖d1+= ½-½ [61] Vachier Lagrave, M [2710] – Koch, J [2483] France 2010.

📖 5

A) 27. ♘e4 e2 28. ♖e1+–

B) 27. ♖f1?? ♖cxd7! 28. ♗xd7 ♕xf1+! 29. ♘xf1 e2∓ 0-1 [43] Efimenko, Z [2702] – Forster, R [2458] Porto Carras 2011.

📖 6

A) 10... ♕xd7! 11. ♗xd6 ♕xd6 12. dxc5 ♕xc5 and if White tries to sacrifice: 13. ♗xh7+ ♔xh7 14. ♕h5+ ♔g8 15. ♘e4 g6 16. ♕g5 ♕e7 17. ♘f6+ ♔g7 18. ♘h5+ ♔h7 19. ♘f6+ ♔g7=

B) 10... ♗xd7? 11. ♗xd6 ♕xd6 12. dxc5 ♕xc5 13. ♗xh7+! ♔xh7 14. ♕h5+ ♔g8 15. ♘e4 ♕c4 *(15... g6 16. ♘xc5 gxh5 17. ♘xd7+– The difference! The Bishop on d7 was hanging!)* 16. ♘g5 ♖fd8

17. ♕xf7+ ♔h8 18. ♕h5+ ♔g8 19. ♖d1± White's position is crushing. 1-0 [30] Kamsky, G [2778] – Shankland, S [2698] USA 2014.

📖 7

A) 51. ♘xg7 ♗xd2 52. ♘xe6 ♗xc1=

B) 51. ♖dd1? ♖g2! The position clearly becomes favourable for Black! 52. ♔xg2 ♕e2+! *(52... ♗e7? 53. ♘xe7 ♕e2+ 54. ♔h1 ♕f3+ 55. ♔h2 ♕f2+ 56. ♔h1 ♕f3+ 57. ♔h2 ♕f2+ ½-½ [57] Karpov, A [2619] – Graf, F [2493] Germany 2014)* 53. ♔g1 ♕xh5 54. ♖h4□ ♕xf5 55. axb3 ♗e7 White is in big trouble, e.g. 56. ♕h2 *(56. ♕f2 ♕h3–+; 56. ♕g3 ♖g6–+)* 56... ♕g4+! *(56... ♖xe3∓)* 57. ♔h1 *(57. ♕g2 ♕h5–+)* 57... ♖xe3 58. ♖g1 ♕f3+ 59. ♖g2 ♗f6–+.

📖 8

A) 17... ♕b6 and Black is only a bit worse.

B) 17... g5? 18. f4!! gxh4 19. fxe5 ♘h7 20. ♕c4+– 1-0 [44] Edouard, R [2639] – Claesen, P [2319] Montreal 2015.

📖 9

A) 30. g4 exd4 31. ♘xd4 ♖f8!?∞

B) 30. h5?? ♗h6 0-1 Mueller, M [2385] – Braun, A [2567] Germany 2016.

📖 10

A) 33. ♖e1! just wins, for example: 33... ♗xe1 34. ♗xb2 ♗a5 35. ♕f5+ g6 36. ♕f3!+– (Δ♖e7).

B) 33. ♖d1?? ♖d2! 34. ♔g2 *(34. ♖xd2?? ♕f1#)* 34... ♖xd1 *(34... ♖e2? 35. ♔h3± ½-½ [41] Jobava, B [2676] – Alekseenko, K [2554] Russia 2016)* 35. ♕xd1 ♗b6=

📖 11

A) 28... ♕b5–+

B) 28... ♖xc5?? 29. ♘xe6 ♖xe5 30. ♕xe5! ♗xe5 31. ♖f8+ ♔h7 32. ♖f7+ ♔g8 33. ♖f8+ ♔h7 34. ♖f7+ ♗g7 35. ♖xg7+ ♔h8 36. ♖h7+! ♔g8 37. ♖g7+ ♔h8 ½-½ [37] Artemiev, V [2674] – Petrosian, T [2607] Russia 2016.

📖 12

A) 32... ♕a2 33. ♖xd8 ♖xd8 34. ♖xd4 ♖e8∓

B) 32... ♕a7?? 33. ♖xd8 ♖xd8 34. ♖xd4! ♕a1+ *(34... ♖e8 35. ♕b3++–)* 35. ♔g2 ♕a8+ 36. ♔g3 1-0 [36] Shirov, A [2689] – Simacek, P [2454] Czech Republic 2016 *(Black resigned in view of: 36. ♔g3 ♖e8 37. ♕e6+! ♖xe6 38. ♖d8+ ♖e8 39. ♖xe8#).*

A) 14... ♖fc8! 15. ♗c3 ♗b5 16. ♕b2 ♗xe2 17. ♗xb4 ♗xf3–+ There is no Rook hanging on f8!

B) 14... ♖ac8? 15. ♗c3 ♗b5 16. ♕b2± 1-0 [49] Sethuraman,S [2658] – Sengupta,D [2554] Dubai 2016 *[16. ♕b2 ♗xe2 17. ♗xb4 ♗xf3?! fails: 18. ♗xf8 ♗xg2 19. ♖g1+–].*

A) 33. ♖xd3! ♖axd3 34. ♗e4+ ♖xe4+ 35. ♔xd3 ♖f4 36. c5 ♖f3+ 37. ♔c4 ♖xh3 38. ♖c8 and the c-pawn will bring White a draw.

B) 33. ♔e3? e5! 34. ♗e4+ ♖xe4+ 35. ♔xe4 ♘c5+! 36. ♔xe5 f6+ 37. ♔d4 *[37. ♔f4? g5+ 38. ♔f5 ♖f3#]* 37... ♘e6+ 38. ♔e4 ♘g5+ 39. ♔d4 *[39. ♔f5 ♖f3#]* 39... ♘f3+–+ 0-1 [47] Schiendorfer, E [2384] – Fischer, M [2085] Switzerland 2016.

A) 24. ♗a3! ♖c2 25. ♘e4! ♕xe4 *[25... ♖ec7?? 26. ♖d8+ ♔f7 27. ♘d6++–]* 26. ♗xe7=

B) 24. ♕xf5?? exf5! *[24... ♖xf5? 25. ♖d8+ ♖e8□ 26. ♗xf6 ♖xd8 27. ♗xd8 ♖f4=]* 25. ♗a3 ♖d5–+ 0-1 [55] Naiditsch, A [2660] – Demuth, A [2550] Germany 2016.

A) 37. ♔e1!±

B) 37. ♔e2? ♖f2+ 38. ♔d3 *[38. ♔d1 ♖d2+ 39. ♔e1 ♗f2+ 40. ♔f1 ♖d1+ 41. ♔e2 ♖e1+ 42. ♔d3 c4+ 43. ♔xc4 ♘d2+–+]* 38... ♖d2+! 39. ♔c4 *[39. ♔xe4 ♖e2+–+]* 39... ♘d6+ 40. ♔d5 ♗f6+–+ 1-0 [67] Edouard, R [2639] – Darini, P [2524] Iran 2016.

A) 26. ♔e1 is about equal, for example: 26... ♘e4 27. ♖c2 ♘f3+ 28. ♔e2 ♘g1+ 29. ♔e1 ♘f3+=

B) 26. ♔e2?? ♘e4 27. ♖d3 *[27. ♖c2 ♖xc1! 28. ♖xc1 ♖d2+ 29. ♔f1 ♖xf2+ 30. ♔e1 ♘f3+ 31. ♔d1 ♖d2#]* 27... ♘xd3 28. ♗xd3 ♘c3+ 29. ♔d2 ♘xa2 0-1 Hammer, J [2652] – Carlstedt, J [2457] Denmark 2016.

A) 52. ♕e5+? ♔h7 53. ♔xh4? ♕f3 54. g5 ♕f2+ 0-1 [54] Xu Xiangyu [2461] – Zhao, C [2096] Shenzhen 2016 *[White resigned in view of: 54... ♕f2+ 55. ♕g3 hxg5+ 56. ♔g4 ♕f5#].*

B) 52. ♕d4+! ♔h7 53. ♔xh4 ♕f3 54. ♖d3 *[54. g5?? hxg5+ 55. ♔xg5 f6+–+]* 54... g5+ 55. ♔h5 ♕c6 56. ♕d6+–

A) <u>64. ♔g3</u> ♖xe2 65. ♖xe2 ♖xe2 66. ♖xb3 ♖c2 67. ♖b6+– Δf5, ♔f4

B) 64. c7?? ♘c1! 65. ♖xc1 *(65. c8=♕?? ♘xd3+ 66. ♔f1 ♘xe1–+)* 65... ♖xe2+ 66. ♔f1 ♖h2 67. ♔g1 ♖ag2+ 68. ♔f1 ♖f2+ 69. ♔g1 ♖hg2+ 70. ♔h1 ♖h2+ ½-½ Mareco, S [2606] – Nakamura, H [2789] Baku 2016.

A) <u>39. ♘c4</u> ♕xa4∞

B) 39. ♗b5?? ♕xb5 40. axb5 ♘e2+–+ 0-1 [60] Cori, J [2609] – Salgado Lopez, I [2662] Baku 2016.

A) 31... ♖a3?? 32. ♖b2!! and the position is a draw: 32... ♖xb3 33. ♖xg2+ ♔h7 *(33... ♔f7?! 34. ♖eg8 ♗f8 35. ♖h8 and Black cannot avoid ♖h7+ and is even worse!)* 34. ♖h2+ ♔g7 35. ♖g2+=

B) <u>31... ♕f7</u> is one of many winning moves. 32. ♕d1 ♘c4–+ Black is of course completely winning, although in the game White somehow won! 1-0 [75] Shankland, S [2679] – Sethuraman, S [2640] Baku 2016.

A) <u>60... ♖xd2</u> 61. ♖xd2 ♖xe5 62. ♕xf7+ ♕xf7 63. gxf7 ♔xf7 with a likely draw although White must still defend accurately!

B) 60... ♖xe5?? 61. ♗h6+! ♔xh6 62. ♖h8+ ♔g7 63. ♖h7+ ♔f8 64. ♖xf7+ ♔e8 65. ♖f8+ ♔e7 66. ♕f6+ ♔d7 67. ♖f7+ ♔e8 *(67... ♔c8 68. ♖xc7++–)* 68. ♕h8# 1-0 Pultinevicius, P – Moroni, L Khanty-Mansiysk 2016.

A) <u>11... ♘xc5!</u> 12. b4 ♕a4 13. ♕xa4+ ♘xa4 14. ♖a2 ♘c3 *(14... ♗d7!? is also possible)* 15. ♖b2 ♘a4=

B) 11... dxc4? 12. e3 ♘b3 13. ♗xc4! ♘xa1 14. b4 ♕d8 15. ♘xe4 0-0 16. ♗b2+– 1-0 [34] Charochkina, D [2366] – Gunina, V [2535] Novosibirsk 2016.

A) <u>14... ♕xd1+</u> is necessary.

B) 14... f5? 15. ♕xd8 ♖xd8 16. c6!+– 1-0 [25] Carlsen, M [2840] – Bosiocic, M [2591] Doha 2016.

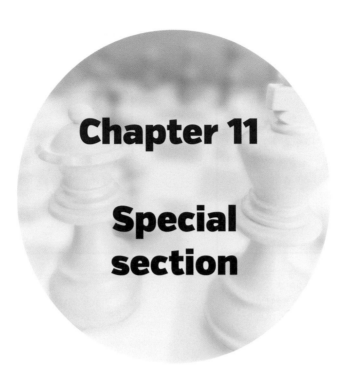

Chapter 11

Special section

In this chapter, you will find all the exercises which need a special introduction or do not fit in any of the other chapters.

Simply follow the instructions!

The difficulty of these exercises ranges from quite easy to difficult. An asterisk indicates that the exercise is more difficult than average.

1

Gupta, A. – Negi, P.

□ 28. ?
What is the best way
to handle this mess?

2

Laznicka, V. – Negi, P.

■
Can Black save the day playing
48...♘xe4 49.♕xe4 ♕f2?

3

Meier, G. – Kramnik, V.

□
Can White save the day
playing 31.♘f6+?

4

Vachier Lagrave, M. – Cruz, C.

■
Black went 29...♖d1 (with the idea
to answer 30.♘e5 with 30...h5).
Was it indeed solving his problems?

5 [*]

Hou, Y. – Kramnik, V.

■ 16... ?
Find an excellent move, granting
Black a great advantage.

6

Baskin, R. – Michalik, P.

□ 30. ?
Find the smart winning move!

📖 7

Haba, P. – Moiseenko, A.

□ 24. ?
Find the crushing move!

📖 8 [*]

Gabuzyan, H. – Edouard, R.

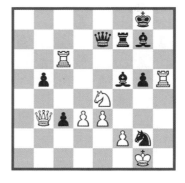

■ 35... ?
Find the winning move!

Vitiugov, N. – Sasikiran, K.

☐
Should White go 27.♖xd4?

Riff, V. – Gantner, M.

■ 33... ?
Find the winning continuation!

Nisipeanu, L. – Batsiashvili, N.

☐ 30. ?
Black seems to be solid:
how can White break through?

Timofeev, A. – Eliseev, U.

☐ 48. ?
How would you manage this mess?

📖 13 (*)

Loiseau, Q. – Fier, A.

□

Which move is winning: 50.♕xh6+,
50.♖e2, 50.♘b5 or 50.♖h2?

📖 14

Stupak, K. – Santos Ruiz, M.

□ 28. ?
Which move breaks Black's
fragile defence?

📖 15 (*)

Tomashevsky, E. – Movsesian, S.

■ 27… ?
Find the winning idea!
Not easy, but not spectacular…

📖 16 (*)

Predke, A. – Safarli, E.

□ 30. ?
White to play and win!
Sophistication is our enemy…
This is the most difficult exercise.

📖 17

Kulaots, K. – Esipenko, A.

■ 48… ?
Find the winning move!

📖 18 (*)

Topalov, V. – Giri, A.

■ 37… ?
How can Black force a draw?

📖 19

Sanders, I. – Edouard, R.

■ 24… ?
A tricky position where both sides are in
danger: find the winning move for Black!

📖 20 (*)

Speelman, J. – Fressinet, L.

■ 32… ?
Find the winning continuation!

21

Steil-Antoni, F. – Stefanova, A.

□
Should White play 41.♖e1, or be
afraid of 41...♖e5 as an answer?

22

Ochsner, B. – Edouard, R.

■ 53... ?
You are in time trouble: find the best
move as quickly as possible!

23

Lai, H. – Bauer, C.

■
Which move is the winning one:
31...♖d6 or 31...♖g6?

24

Edouard, R. – Stremavicius, T.

□ 16. ?
White to escape that mess, and win!

25

Vachier-Lagrave, M. – Topalov, V.

☐ 25. ?
Find the way to a huge advantage!

26

Karjakin, S. – Shoker, S.

■ 27… ?
Black seems to be losing material…
but with the help of a brillant move,
he is in fact better! Spot this move!

27 (*)

Sargissian, G. – Pourramezanali, A.

☐ 35. ?
Black's King has insufficient protection:
how would you continue your attack?

28

Firouzja, A. – Edouard, R.

☐
If White goes 30.♗c1
should Black play 30…b2?

📖 29

Carlsen, M. – Giri, A.

□ 23. ?
Which elegant way of winning
material did the World Champion miss?

📖 30

Shankland, S. – Pfreundt, J.

□ 10.dxe5?
Should White go for the e5-pawn?

📖 31

Daly, C. – Morris, C.

□ 24. ?
Anything better than 24.♗c3?

📖 32 [*]

Topalov, V. – Caruana, F.

■ 30... ?
Black to play... and be clearly better!

📖 33

Dominguez Perez, L. – Aronian, L.

■ 25... ?
Can Black save the game?

📖 34

Bok, B. – Grischuk, A.

■ 26... ?
Pick the best move!

📖 35

Bauer, C. – Schroeder, J.

□ 24. ?
Find the crushing move!

📖 36 (*)

Sokolov, I. – Swapnil, S.

■ 29... ?
Find the winning move and its continuation. Black must find
several accurate moves to win!

📖 37

Ivanov, S. – Sokolov, I.

□ 52. ?
A tricky position:
how should White deal with it?

📖 38

Wei, Y. – Nepomniachtchi, I.

□ 25. ?
White has one way to an advantage:
find it!

📖 39

Gelfand, B. – Steinberg, N.

□ 32. ?
How can White make use of his d-pas-
ser?

📖 40

Maze, S. – Kobo, O.

□ 32. ?
Find the only winning move!

SOLUTIONS – CHAPTER 11

📖 1

28. ♖xd4! cxd4 [28... ♖xd4 29. ♘xe5 ♗xc2 30. ♖xc2+−] **29. ♕xc8+−** 1-0 [31] Gupta, A [2580] – Negi, P [2618] Dubai 2011.

📖 2

48... ♘xe4 49. ♕xe4 ♕f2

No! This is indeed the only try, but it fails...

50. ♕f5+ [=50. ♕e5+ ♔h4 51. ♕e7+ f6 52. ♕xf6+] **50... ♔h4 51. ♕f6+!!** ♔h5 [51... gxf6 52. ♖xh6#] **52. ♕xf7+** ♔h4 **53. ♕e7+** 1-0 Laznicka,V [2681] – Negi,P [2622] India 2011.

Black resigned in view of: 53. ♕e7+ ♔h5 54. ♕c5++−.

📖 3

32. ♘f6+

No! Let's see why...

32... ♕xf6!! 33. ♕xd5 [33. gxf6 ♘f4+ 34. ♔f1 ♖b1+−+] **33... ♕g6 34. ♕e5 ♖b5−+** 0-1 [38] Meier, G [2610] – Kramnik, V [2784] Dortmund 2013.

📖 4

29... ♖d1

No! Let's see why...

30. ♔f3!! ♖d2 [30... ♖xd3?! 31. ♔e2+−] **31. gxf5 h5 32. ♗f1+−** 1-0 [47] Vachier Lagrave, M [2722] – Cruz, C [2529] Linares 2013.

📖 5

16... ♘c5!!

Keeping the bishop pair and activity, while the a8-Rook is untouchable.

17. ♕xa8

A] 17. b4 ♗b7 18. ♕xe6 ♘xe6∓ 0-1 [28] Hou, Y [2676] – Kramnik, V [2783] Dortmund 2015.

B] 17. ♕xe6 ♗xe6−+

17... ♗b7

Black's pieces are way too strong!

18. ♕a3 [18. ♕a7 ♖a8−+] **18... ♗xf3! 19. gxf3** [19. c4 ♘h4−+; 19. ♕b4 ♘f4−+] **19... ♘h4 20. ♔h1** [20. ♖d1 ♕h3−+] **20... ♘d3 21. ♖f1 ♕h3−+**

📖 6

30. ♖c7! [△♕xh4]

Simple chess! Instead, the game continued: 30. ♕xh4 ♖xd6 31. ♖ee1± ½-½ (38) Baskin, R (2369) – Michalik, P (2574) Germany 2016.

30... ♖xf4 31. ♕e3 ♕e4 32. ♕b6 ♖e8 33. d7+–

📖 7

24. ♖xd4! ♘xd4 [24... exd4? 25. ♕xe6++–] **25. ♕xe5+–** ½-½ (31) Haba, P (2487) – Moiseenko, A (2673) Germany 2016.

📖 8

35... ♘xe3!!

Instead, the game continued: 35... ♗xe4? 36. ♖c8+ ♗f8 37. dxe4 ♘h4 38. ♕xc3∞ ½-½ (53) Gabuzyan, H (2585) – Edouard, R (2627) Al Ain 2015.

36. fxe3 [36. ♖xc3 ♘c4!–+] **36... ♕a7!–+** and White cannot hold both the e3-pawn and his e4-knight.

📖 9

27. ♖xd4!

Yes!

📖 [continued]

27... ♘xd4 28. ♕xd4+ f6 29. ♘c7!± A little trick making the whole idea work! 1-0 (42) Vitiugov, N (2724) – Sasikiran, K (2638) Doha 2015.

📖 10

33... ♗xe4 34. ♖xe4 [34. dxe4 ♖xc4–+] **34... ♖b1+ 35. ♔g2 ♖xf2+!** The unexpected blow! **36. ♔xf2 ♕f8+ 37. ♖f4** [37. ♔e2 ♕f1+ 38. ♔d2 ♕d1#] **37... ♗xf4 38. ♔g2** [38. gxf4 ♕xf4+ 39. ♔g2 ♖e1!–+; 38. ♕f3 ♗e3+ 39. ♔e2 ♖e1+–+] **38... ♗e3–+** 0-1 (40) Riff, V (2372) – Gantner, M (2274) Switzerland 2015.

Black had many winning moves, 38... ♗xg3!? being one of them.

📖 11

30. f5! gxf5 31. ♗xf5 ♖d6 [31... ♔xf5? 32. ♖f3#] **32. ♗xh7+–** 1-0 (49) Nisipeanu, L (2679) – Batsiashvili, N (2485) Wijk aan Zee 2016.

📖 12

48. ♕xe5! 1-0 Timofeev, A (2570) – Eliseev, U (2582) Russia 2016.

Black resigned in view of: 48. ♕xe5 ♕xe5 *[48... ♖xg8 49. ♕b8++–]* 49. ♕xf7#.

50. 🖤e2‼

A) 50. ♕xh6+? 🖤h7 51. 🖤e2 *[51. ♕d6 🖤xd7 52. 🖤h2+ ♔g8 53. ♕g6+ ♔g7 54. ♕e6+ 🖤f7 55. ♘d5 ♔f8 56. ♕h6+ ♔g8= ½-½ [73] Loiseau, Q [2437] – Fier Takeda, A [2608] France 2016]* 51... 🖤xh6 52. 🖤e8+ ♔g7 53. 🖤xd8 🖤d6 54. ♘b5 🖤d5 55. ♘c7 ♗f6!=

B) 50. ♘b5? 🖤xd7 *[50... ♔xd7 51. ♕xh6+ ♔g8 52. ♘xd4 cxd4 53. b4±]* 51. ♕xh6+ 🖤h7 52. ♕c6 ♕f8 53. ♘xd4 cxd4 54. 🖤xd4±

C) 50. 🖤h2? ♕xd7 51. 🖤xh6+ ♔g8=

50... 🖤xd7 *[50... 🖤xe2 51. ♘xe2+− △♘f4]* **51. ♕xh6+ ♔g8** *[51... 🖤h7 52. ♕g6! 🖤h1+ 53. ♔c2+−]* **52. ♕e6+! 🖤f7 53. ♘b5! ♔f8 54. ♘xd4! ♕xd4** *[54... cxd4? 55. ♕h6++−]* **55. ♕e8+ ♔g7 56. 🖤g2+ ♔f6 57. ♕h8+ ♔e6 58. 🖤e2+ ♔d6** *[58... ♔d5 59. 🖤d2! ♕xd2 60. ♕d8++−; 58... ♔f5 59. ♕h5+ ♔f6 60. ♕h6+ ♔f5 61. ♕e6++−]* **59. ♕d8+ ♔c6 60. 🖤e6+ ♔b5 61. ♕b6+ ♔c4 62. ♕a6+ ♔d5 63. 🖤d6++−**

28. ♘h6+! ♔h8 *[28... gxh6 29. ♗xf6+−]* **29. ♗xf6** 1-0 Stupak, K [2537] – Santos Ruiz, M [2418] Spain 2016.

Black resigned in view of: 29. ♗xf6 gxf6 30. ♕xd8+ ♕xd8 31. ♘xf7++−.

27... 🖤xe4!

27... 🖤xf2? 28. ♗xd4 🖤xe4?? *[28... cxd4 29. 🖤xh2 🖤xh2+ 30. ♔xh2 ♕f4+∞]* 29. ♗xf2 c4 30. ♕f3 1-0 Tomashevsky, E [2728] – Movsesian, S [2653] China 2016.

28. ♘xe4 *[28. ♕xe4 ♕xh3−+]* **28... 🖤f3!** Simple chess! **29. 🖤xf3 ♘xf3−+** E.g. **30. ♘f6** [30. ♕d8+ ♔h7 31. ♗xg7 ♕xg7 32. ♘f6+ ♔h6 33. 🖤d1 ♗f7−+; 30. ♘d2 ♕h3−+] **30... gxf6 31. ♗xf6+ ♔g8 32. ♕d5+ ♔h7 33. ♕xb7+ ♔h6−+**

30. ♘g5+!

Instead, the game went: 30. c3? ♕a-2!?⇆ ½-½ [46] Predke, A [2508] – Safarli, E [2663] Russia 2016.

30... ♔g6 31. ♗xd4 ♕xd4

31... ♔xg5 32. 🖤g1++−

32. ♔b1‼+−

White is winning. Some examples...

32... ♕xc5

A) 32... ♕g4 33. 🖤g3+−

B) 32... ♕f4 33. 🖤g1 ♕xf2 34. ♘h3++−

C) 32... ♔f6 33. 🖤f3+ ♔e7 34. 🖤f7+ ♔e8 35. 🖤e1+ ♔d8 36. ♘e6++−

D) 32... ♔xg5 33. ♖g3++−

33. ♖g1 ♕b5+

A) 33... ♕b6+ 34. ♔a2 ♖c8 35. ♖e6++−

B) 33... ♔f5 34. ♖f3+ ♔e5 35. ♘f7+ *(35. ♖e1+ ♔d6 36. h7+−)* 35... ♔e4 36. ♖xg8 ♔xf3 37. ♖g3+ ♔xf2 38. ♖b3+− ∆h7

34. ♔a1 ♖c8 35. ♖f3+− *(∆♘f7+)*

Also winning is 35. ♘e4+!?+−.

📖 17

48... ♖h1+! 0-1 Kulaots, K [2578] – Esipenko, A [2445] Russia 2016.

Black resigned in view of: 48... ♖h1+ 49. ♔xh1 fxe2−+.

Instead, 48... fxe2? would fail to: 49. ♘ce7 ♖h1+ 50. ♔g2 ♖g1+ 51. ♔h2=.

📖 18

37... ♖xh2!! 38. ♖xd7 *(38. ♔xh2? ♕xc7∓)* **38... ♖h1+ 39. ♔f2 ♖h2+ 40. ♔g2 ♖xg2+ 41. ♔f1 ♖h2! 42. ♖d2 ♖h1+ 43. ♔f2 ♖h2+=** ½-½ [45] Topalov,V [2754] – Giri,A [2790] Norway 2016.

📖 19

24... ♕h5! 25. ♗f2 *(25. cxd4 ♗b5+−; 25. ♔e1 d3−+)* **25... ♗b5+ 26. ♔g1 ♕xh2#** 0-1 Sanders, I [2326] – Edouard, R [2632] England 2016.

📖 20

32... ♕c5+!

32... ♕b6+? 33. c5 ♕xc5+∓ 1-0 [41] Speelman, J [2517] – Friedgood, D [2692] England 2016.

33. ♔h2 *(33. ♔h1 e4! 34. ♗xe4 ♗xe4 35. fxe4 ♕h5+ 36. ♔g1 g3−+)* **33... e4! 34. ♗xe4 ♗xe4 35. fxe4** *(35. ♕xe4 ♕d6+−+)* **35... ♕d6+! 36. e5** *(36. ♔g1 ♕b6+ 37. ♔h1 ♕h6+ 38. ♔g1 g3−+)* **36... ♕h6+ 37. ♔g3** *(37. ♔g1 g3−+)* **37... ♕e3+ 38. ♔xg4** *(38. ♔h2 ♖d3−+)* **38... ♖d3!−+**

📖 21

41. ♖e1!

This move should be played!

Instead, the game went: 41. ♖f3+? ♔e5 42. ♖e3+ ♔d6 43. ♕xh5 ♖e5⇆ 0-1 [48] Steil Antoni, F [2150] – Stefanova, A [2519] England 2016.

41... ♖e5 Indeed the most consistent defence, but failing. **42. ♕xh5! ♖xe1 43. ♕f7+! ♕xf7 44. exf7+−**

📖 22

53... f5!

Instead, the game continued: 53... b2? 54. ♔g2? *(△ 54. ♕e7)* 54... ♖e3 55. ♖xb2 ♕c8 56. f5? *(△56. ♔h2)* 56... ♕c6+ 57. ♔h2 ♕d6+ 58. ♔h1 ♖h3+

0-1 Ochsner, B [2397] – Edouard, R [2641] Mallorca 2016.

54. g5+ (54. ♕e7 ♕b2+−+) **54... ♔h5−+**

📖 23

31... ♖d6!

31... ♖g6? 32. ♗h3 ♕xe2 33. ♕xe2 ♗xg3+ 34. ♔g1 ♗f2+ 35. ♔h2 ♗g3+ 36. ♔g1 ½-½ Lai, H [2332] – Bauer, C [2634] Netherlands 2016.

32. ♕f3 (32. ♕xe4+ ♗xe4 33. ♖xd6 ♗xg2 34. ♔xg2 ♗c5−+) **32... ♗xg3+!** **33. ♘xg3 ♕xh4+ 34. ♗h3** (34. ♔g1 ♘xg3−+) **34... ♕xh3+! 35. ♔xh3 ♘g5+ 36. ♔h4 ♘xf3+ 37. ♔h3 ♖g6−+**

📖 24

16. ♘d1! ♕xa1 17. ♕g6! ♗xe5 18. ♕xg8+ ♔d7 19. ♕xa8+− 1-0 [30] Edouard, R [2641] – Stremavicius, T [2443] Mallorca 2016.

📖 25

25. ♕g3!

25. d7?? ♘xe1? (25... ♖d8! 26. ♖d1 ♘xc1 27. ♘c6? ♘e2+−+) 26. dxc8=♕+ ♕xc8 27. ♕g3 ♔h8 28. h4? (28. ♗h6! gxh6 29. ♕e5+±) 28... ♘d3∞ ½-½ [66] Vachier Lagrave, M [2789] – Topalov, V [2761] Paris 2016.

25... ♔h8 (25... ♘xe1 26. ♗h6 g6 27. ♕e5+−) **26. ♖e3!** (26. ♖d1!? is also very strong) **26... ♘xc1 27. d7 ♖d8 28. ♕xb8 ♖xb8 29. ♘c6+−**

📖 26

27... ♘d4!!

Black is suddenly much better. Let's see some examples how this can develop...

28. ♕g4

A) 28. cxd4 ♗xd4 29. ♖f1 ♕b3 30. ♖a3 ♖xf2! 31. ♖xf2 ♖d1+−+

B) 28. ♕f1 ♖b6! Going for a win! (28... ♘b3 29. ♗e3⇆) 29. ♖a4 (29. ♗e3 ♕b3! 30. ♖xa6 ♘c2−+) 29... ♘b3 30. ♗g5 ♘d2 31. ♕e2 ♘xe4−+

28... ♕b3 (28... ♖df3!? or 28... ♘c2!? are also very strong) **29. ♖xa6** (△ 29. e5 ♖df3!?∓) **29... ♕c2** (29... h5!?−+) **30. ♖f1** (30. ♘xd3 cxd3−+) **30... ♘e2+−+** 0-1 [33] Karjakin, S [2774] – Shoker, S [2489] Kazakhstan 2016.

📖 27

35. ♖e1+!

35. ♕h5+? ♔d7 (35... ♔f8!? 36. ♕h6+ ♔f7=) 36. ♖d1 ♖xg2+ 37. ♔f1 ♖d2! 38. ♕h7+ ♔c8 39. ♕h8+ ♔d7= ½-½ [47] Sargissian, G [2679] – Pourramezanali, A [2509] Iran 2016.

35... ♚d8 36. ♖e2!

Simple chess! The black King cannot escape.

36... ♚c8 [36... ♕xc5+ 37. ♔h1 ♖f8 38. ♖d2+ ♚c8 39. ♕d7+ ♚b8 40. ♖c2+–] **37. ♗e5 ♕xc5+ 38. ♔h2 ♖f8 39. ♖e3+–** The easiest [Δ♖c3].

📖 28

30. ♗c1

Instead, the game continued: 30. ♖e1 b2 31. ♖b1 ♖c8∓ Δ...♘c4: 0-1 [33] Firouzja, A [2481] – Edouard, R [2639] Iran 2016.

30... b2

Yes! Black is winning.

31. ♗xb2 ♕xb2 32. ♕xd6? ♕a1+! 33. ♔g2 ♕a8+–+

📖 29

23. c5!

In the game Magnus only obtained an initiative: 23. cxd5? exd5 24. ♘b3 ♕xc2 25. ♘d4↑ 1-0 [45] Carlsen, M [2855] – Giri, A [2785] Bilbao 2016.

23... bxc5 24. ♖a6± [Δ♖xd6]

📖 30

10. dxe5!

Yes!

10... dxe5 11. ♕xd8 ♖axd8 [11... ♖fxd8 12. ♘xe5 ♗xe4 13. ♘xe4 ♘xe4 14. ♘d3 f5 15. f3 ♗c5+ 16. ♔f1+–] **12. ♘xe5 ♗xe4 13. ♘xe4 ♘xe4 14. ♘d3! f5 15. f3 ♗c5+ 16. ♘xc5!** [16. ♔f1? ♗b6=] **16... ♘xc5 17. ♗g5!** A theoretical trick! **17... ♖d5 18. ♗e7 ♖e8 19. c4+–** 1-0 [25] Shankland, S [2661] – Pfreundt, J [2292] Biel 2016.

📖 31

24. a3!!

Stronger than 24. ♗c3? only winning a pawn, while in the game White went wrong with 24. c3?? ♕a3⇆ ½-½ [50] Daly, C [2328] – Morris, C [2127] Baku 2016.

24... ♕xa3 25. ♗b2 ♕b4 26. ♖d4+–

📖 32

30... ♖xg7!

Instead, the game went: 30... ♗xc3? 31. bxc3 ♕b2∞ 0-1 [38] Topalov, V [2760] – Caruana, F [2823] London 2016.

31. ♗xd4 [31. ♖xg7? ♖h8!–+] **31... ♖xg5 32. ♗xb6+ ♚xb6∓** White is in big danger: his Knight on a3 is very limited and the d3-pawn is powerful.

25... ♞d2

No! This move is the only try, but fails...

26. ♕xf7+! (26. ♖xe7?? ♖xe7 27. ♕xc5 ♖e1+ 28. ♔h2 ♞f1+=) **26... ♕xf7 27. ♖xe8++−** 1-0 Dominguez Perez,L [2739] – Aronian,L [2785] Doha 2016.

26... ♕g5! 27. ♕xf4 (27. g3 ♞h3+−+) **27... ♕xf4−+** 0-1 [45] Bok, B [2598] – Grischuk, A [2737] Doha 2016.

24. ♞h4! ♗e5 25. ♖d7! ♗xb2 26. ♞xg6! ♗xf6 27. ♞xf8+ ♔xf8 28. ♖xc7+− 1-0 [40] Bauer, C [2635] – Schroeder, J [2541] Zurich 2016.

29... ♕e2! 30. ♖xb1 ♖xb1+ 31. ♔h2 ♕d1! [31... ♕xe4?? 32. ♗xg7+−] **32. ♖xg7+ ♗xg7 33. ♗xg7 ♕h1+ 34. ♔g3 ♗xh3!** Otherwise White would escape. **35. ♗xh6** (35. gxh3 ♕xe4−+) **35... ♕xg2+ 36. ♔f4 f5 37. ♞f6+ ♔f7 38. ♕e3 ♕h2+−+** 0-1 [40] Sokolov, I [2632] – Swapnil, S [2526] Stockholm 2017.

52. ♗e5!+−

≤ 52. ♗c3? ♕d5+= ½-½ [63] Ivanov, S [2545] – Sokolov, I [2632] Sweden 2017.

52... d2 53. ♕e6 d1=♕ [53... ♕g8 54. ♗xg7+ ♕xg7 55. ♕e8+ ♕g8 56. ♕xe3+−] **54. ♗xg7+ ♔xg7 55. ♕f7+ ♔h8 56. ♕h7#**

25. ♕xd7+ ♔xd7 26. e6+!! fxe6 [26... ♔xe6? 27. ♖xe4++−] **27. ♖f7 ♖g5□** [27... ♖ae8 28. ♖d1++−] **28. ♖d1+** [=28. ♗xg5] **28... ♔e8 29. ♖h7±/±** 1-0 [75] Wei Yi [2706] – Nepomniachtchi, I [2767] Wijk aan Zee 2017.

32. d7 ♖d8 33. ♖c8! 1-0 Gelfand, B [2721] – Steinberg, N [2486] Gibraltar 2017.

Black resigned in view of: 33. ♖c8 ♖xc8 34. ♕g4++−.

32. ♖d7! [32. ♖f1? ♕d2!?⩱; 32. ♖d5 ♗h6⩱] **32... ♕c1+ 33. ♔h2 ♖xe3** [33... ♗e5+? 34. ♗xe5 ♖xc6 35. ♖d8+ ♔h7 36. ♖h8#] **34. ♕d5+−** White ends up with an extra pawn and initiative! 1-0 [44] Maze, S [2613] – Kobo, O [2482] Gibraltar 2017.

To come soon...

CHESS CALCULATION TRAINING

Volume 2

Endgames!

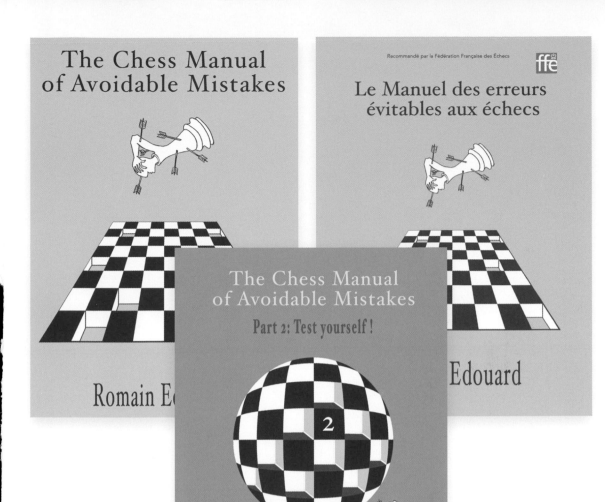

The Chess Manual
of Avoidable Mistakes

Le Manuel des erreurs
évitables aux échecs

Recommandé par la Fédération Française des Échecs

ffé

Romain E̶... Edouard

The Chess Manual
of Avoidable Mistakes

Part 2: Test yourself !

2

Romain Edouard

Thinkers Publishing

www.thinkerspublishing.com